ROYAL COURT

Royal Court Theatre presents

DISCONNECT

by **Anupama Chandrasekhar**

First performance at the Royal Court Jerwood Theatre Upstairs, Sloane Square, London on 17th February 2010.

First performance at Elephant and Castle shopping centre as part of the Theatre Local season on 31st March 2010.

DISCONNECT is presented as part of International Playwrights:
A Genesis Foundation Project

DISCONNECT

by **Anupama Chandrasekhar**

Cast
in order of appearance
Avinash **Paul Bhattacharjee**
Jyothi **Hasina Haque**
Vidya **Ayesha Dharker**
Giri **Neet Mohan**
Ross **Nikesh Patel**

Director **Indhu Rubasingham**
Designer **John Napier**
Lighting Designer **Oliver Fenwick**
Sound Designer **David McSeveney**
Casting Director **Amy Ball**
Production Manager **Tariq Rifaat**
Stage Managers **Bryony Drury, Ruth Murfitt**
Costume Supervisor **Iona Kenrick**
Fight Arranger **Bret Yount**
Stage Management Work Placement **Lucy Topham**
Scenic Artists **Charlotte Gainey, Jodie Pritchard**
Set built by **RCT Stage Department**

The Royal Court and Stage Management wish to thank the following for their help with this production: Andrews Office Furniture, Cad dot Services, Fly Davis, Dolce & Gabbana, Ferjani Daikhi, Party Ark Ltd, Party Packs, Zoe Donegan, Catrin Martin, Motley Theatre Design Course, National Enquirer, The Norbury Bedding & Furnishing Centre, Plantronics, Royal Shakespeare Company.

THE COMPANY

ANUPAMA CHANDRASEKHAR (Writer)

FOR THE ROYAL COURT: Free Outgoing, Whiteout (Royal Court 50th Anniversary reading/BBC World Service), Kabaddi-Kabaddi (International Season/Human Rights Watch International Film Festival 2004)

OTHER THEATRE INCLUDES: Acid (Writers' Bloc Festival of New Writing, Mumbai); Closer Apart (Chennai); Anytime Anywhere (Bangalore).

AWARDS INCLUDE: Shortlisted for the Evening Standard Charles Wintour Award for Most Promising Playwright, and for the Susan Smith Blackburn Prize and John Whiting Award for Free Outgoing. Regional Winner Asia of the Commonwealth Short Story Competition 2006.

Anupama is a Chennai based playwright. She attended the Royal Court International Residency on a British Council-Charles Wallace Trust of India fellowship in 2000 and Royal Court workshops in Mumbai from 2002 to 2003.

PAUL BHATTACHARJEE (Avinash)

FOR THE ROYAL COURT: Credible Witness, Blood, Iranian Nights, Lalita's Way, Mohair, The Burrow.

OTHER THEATRE INCLUDES: Arabian Nights, Edward III, The Island Princess, The Malcontent, The Roman Actor(RSC); The Great Game, Guantanamo, Fashion (Tricycle); A Disappearing Number (Complicite - Barbican/World Tour); Playing with Fire, Murmuring Judges (National); Blood Wedding (Almeida); Twelfth Night (Albery); The Mayor of Zalamea (Liverpool Everyman); Hobson's Choice (Young Vic); Arabian Nights (Young Vic/World Tour); Seagull, Present Laughter, The Tempest, A Perfect Ganesh (West Yorkshire Playhouse); Indian Ink (Aldwych); Yes, Memsahib, Inkalaab 1919, Vilayat, England, Your England, Sacrifice, The Lion's Raj, Ancestral Voices, Meet Me, Chilli In Your Eyes, The Little Clay Cart, The Broken Thigh, Abduction Of Draupadi, Exile In The Forest, Bicharo, Sweet Dreams (Tara Arts 1979-97).

TELEVISION INCLUDES: Eastenders, Britz, Waking the Dead, New Tricks, Spooks, The Bill, Bedtime, Rosemary & Thyme, The Jury, Hawk, Navy in Action, Thieftakers, Wing and a Prayer, Turning World, Two Oranges and a Mango, Inkalaab, Ancestral Voices, Chilli in Your Eyes, Johnny Jarvis, Pravina's Wedding, Maigret, Albion Market, Lovebirds, Shalom, Salaam, Bergerac, Here is the News, Saracen, Northern Crescent, Black and Blue, Clubland, Sister Wife, A Summer Day's Dream.

FILM INCLUDES: Casino Royale, White Teeth, Dirty Pretty Things, Jinnah, Wild West.

RADIO INCLUDES: Silver Street.

AYESHA DHARKER (Vidya)

THEATRE INCLUDES: Arabian Nights (RSC); Dr Faustus (Bristol Old Vic); Bombay Dreams (West End/Broadway); The Ramayana (National/Birmingham Rep); Final Solutions (NCPA, Mumbai).

TELEVISION INCLUDES: Coronation Street, Bodies, Waking the Dead, Life Isn't All Ha Ha Hee Hee, Doctor Who, The Commander, Cutting It, Doctors, The House Across the Street, Mysteries of the Dark Jungle.

FILM INCLUDES: Outsourced, Colour Me Kubrick, Mystic Masseur, Star Wars II: Attack of the Clones, The Terrorist, Mistress of Spices, Anita & Me, Mumbai Chaka Chak, Red Alert, Loins of Punjab Presents, Mad, Sad and Bad, Arabian Nights, Split Wide Open, Saaz, City of Joy, Manika une vie plus tard. Shorts: Hideous Man, The Lady Behaves, India Belongs To Me, Jubilee.

OLIVER FENWICK (Lighting Designer)

RECENT THEATRE INCLUDES: The Line (Arcola); The Drunks, The Grain Store, Julius Caesar (RSC); Hedda Gabler (Gate Theatre Dublin); Happy Now?(National); Private Lives, The Giant, Glass Eels, Comfort Me With Apples (Hampstead); If There Is I Haven't Found it Yet, The Contingency Plan (Bush); Mary Stewart (Sweden); Lady from the Sea, She Stoops to Conquer (Birmingham Rep); Kean (Apollo); Solid Gold Cadillac (Garrick); The Secret Rapture (Lyric, West End); Pure Gold (Soho) Henry V ,Mirandolina ,A Convseration (Royal Exchange);Restoration (Headlong); My Fair Lady (Cameron Mackintosh/National Theatre Tour Production); The Caretaker, Comedy of Errors, Bird Calls, The Elephant Man, Iphigenia (Crucible, Sheffield); Endgame, Noises Off, All My Son's, Dr. Faustus (Liverpool Playhouse); The Doll's House (West Yorkshire Playhouse); Far from the Madding Crowd (ETT); Sunshine on Leith (Dundee Rep & Tour); Heartbreak House (Watford Palace); A Model Girl (Greenwich Theatre); The Chairs (Gate); Follies, Insignificance, Breaking the Code (Theatre Royal, Northampton); Tartuffe, The Gentleman From Olmedo, The Venetian Twins, Hobson's Choice, Dancing at Lughnasa, Love in a Maze (Watermill Theatre); Fields of Gold, Villette (Stephen Joseph Theatre); Cinderella (Bristol Old Vic); Hysteria, Children Of A Lesser God (Salisbury Playhouse).

OPERA INCLUDES: Samson et Delilah, Lohengrin (Royal Opera House); The Trojan Trilogy, The Nose (Linbury ROH); The Gentle Giant (The Clore ROH); The Threepenny Opera (The Opera Group); L'Opera Seria (Batignano Festival).

HASINA HAQUE (Jyothi)

THEATRE INCLUDES: All's Well That Ends Well, England People Very Nice (National).

TELEVISION INCLUDES: Albert's Memorial.

DAVID McSEVENEY (Sound Designer)

FOR THE ROYAL COURT: Cock, A Miracle, Shades, The Stone, The Girlfriend Experience (&Theatre Royal Plymouth & Young Vic), Contractions, Fear & Misery/War & Peace.

OTHER THEATRE INCLUDES: Gaslight (Old Vic); Charley's Aunt, An Hour and a Half Late (Theatre Royal Bath); A Passage to India, After Mrs Rochester, Madame Bovary (Shared Experience); Men Should Weep, Rookery Nook (Oxford Stage Company); Othello (Southwark Playhouse).

AS ASSISTANT DESIGNER: The Permanent Way (Out of Joint); My Brilliant Divorce, Auntie and Me (West End); Accidental Death of an Anarchist (Donmar).

ORIGINAL MUSIC: The BFG (Secret Theatre Productions).

David is Head of Sound at the Royal Court.

NEET MOHAN (Giri)

FOR THE ROYAL COURT: The Skriker (Caryl Churchill's 70th Birthday Reading).

OTHER THEATRE INCLUDES: The Fastest Clock in the Universe (Hampstead/Leicester Curve); England People Very Nice (National); Twelfth Night, Romeo & Juliet (Regent's Park Open Air Theatre); Mercury Fur (Paines Plough).

TELEVISION INCLUDES: Psychoville.

JOHN NAPIER (Designer)

THEATRE INCLUDES: Equus (West End/Broadway); Burning Blue, Time, Children of Eden (West End); Skellig (Young Vic); Aladdin (Old Vic); Macbeth, The Comedy of Errors, King Lear, Once in a Lifetime, The Greeks, Nicholas Nickleby, Hedda Gabler, Peter Pan, Mother Courage (RSC); The Party, Equus, Trelawny of the 'Wells', An Enemy of the People, Peter Pan, Candide, South Pacific (National); The Tower, Who's Afraid of Virginia Wolf ?(Almeida); Martin Guerre (West Yorkshire Playhouse).

MUSICAL THEATRE INCLUDES: Jane Eyre (Broadway); Jesus Christ Superstar, Cats, Starlight Express, Les Misérables, Miss Saigon, Sunset Boulevard (West End/Broadway/World Tours); Siegfried & Roy Show (Mirage, Las Vegas).

OPERA INCLUDES: Lohengrin, Macbeth (Royal Opera House); Idomeneo (Glyndebourne); The Devils (E.N.O.); Nabucco (Metropolitan Opera).

FILM INCLUDES: Hook.

AWARDS INCLUDE: Two Society of West End Theatre awards, an Olivier, a BAFTA, and five Tony Awards for Nicholas Nickleby, Cats, Starlight Express, Les Misérables, and Sunset Boulevard. John is a member of the American Academy of Achievement, was elected Royal Designer for Industry in 1996 and is an Honorary Fellow of the London Institute. He is also an Associate Designer of the Royal Shakespeare Company.

NIKESH PATEL (Ross)

Nikesh will be making his professional stage debut in Disconnect.

INDHU RUBASINGHAM (Director)

FOR THE ROYAL COURT: Free Outgoing (& Traverse, Edinburgh Festival Fringe 2008), Sugar Mummies, Clubland, Lift Off, The Crutch.

OTHER THEATRE INCLUDES: Detaining Justice, The Great Game, Darfur, Fabulation, Starstruck (Tricycle); Wuthering Heights (Birmingham Rep); Pure Gold (Soho); Heartbreak House (Watford); The Morris (Liverpool Everyman); Yellowman (Hampstead/Liverpool Everyman); Anna in the Tropics (Hampstead); Romeo & Juliet (Chichester Festival Theatre); The Misanthrope, The Secret Rapture (The Minerva, Chichester); The Waiting Room (National); The Ramayana (National/Birmingham Repertory); Time of Fire, Kaahini (Birmingham Repertory); A River Sutra (Three Mill Island Studios); Shakuntala, Sugar Dollies (Gate); The No Boys' Cricket Club, Party Girls, D'Yer Eat With Yer Fingers?! And D'Yer Eat With Yer Finger?! - The Remix (Theatre Royal Stratford East); A Doll's House (Young Vic Studio); Rhinoceros (UC Davies, California).

OPERA INCLUDES: Another America (Sadler's Wells).

Positions of Associate Director held at The Gate Theatre, Birmingham Rep Theatre and the Young Vic. Also Asociate Director on Bombay Dreams.

THE ENGLISH STAGE COMPANY
AT THE ROYAL COURT

*'For me the theatre is really a religion or way of life.
You must decide what you feel the world is about and
what you want to say about it, so that everything in
the theatre you work in is saying the same thing ... A
theatre must have a recognisable attitude. It will have
one, whether you like it or not.'*

George Devine, first artistic director of the
English Stage Company: notes for an unwritten
book.

photo: Stephen Cummiskey

As Britain's leading national company dedicated to new work, the Royal Court Theatre produces new plays
of the highest quality, working with writers from all backgrounds, and addressing the problems and
possibilities of our time.

"The Royal Court has been at the centre of British cultural life for the past 50 years, an engine room for
new writing and constantly transforming the theatrical culture." Stephen Daldry

Since its foundation in 1956, the Royal Court has presented premieres by almost every leading
contemporary British playwright, from John Osborne's Look Back in Anger to Caryl Churchill's A Number
and Tom Stoppard's Rock 'n' Roll. Just some of the other writers to have chosen the Royal Court to
premiere their work include Edward Albee, John Arden, Richard Bean, Samuel Beckett, Edward Bond,
Leo Butler, Jez Butterworth, Martin Crimp, Ariel Dorfman, Stella Feehily, Christopher Hampton, David Hare,
Eugène Ionesco, Ann Jellicoe, Terry Johnson, Sarah Kane, David Mamet, Martin McDonagh, Conor McPherson,
Joe Penhall, Mark Ravenhill, Simon Stephens, Wole Soyinka, Polly Stenham, David Storey, Debbie Tucker
Green, Arnold Wesker and Roy Williams.

"It is risky to miss a production there." Financial Times

In addition to its full-scale productions, the Royal Court also facilitates international work at a grass roots
level, developing exchanges which bring young writers to Britain and sending British writers, actors and
directors to work with artists around the world. The research and play development arm of the Royal
Court Theatre, The Studio, finds the most exciting and diverse range of new voices in the UK. The Studio
runs play-writing groups including the Young Writers Programme, Critical Mass for black, Asian and minority
ethnic writers and the biennial Young Writers Festival. For further information, go to
www.royalcourttheatre.com/ywp.

"Yes, the Royal Court is on a roll. Yes, Dominic Cooke has just the genius and kick that this venue needs...
It's fist-bitingly exciting." Independent

Supported by
**ARTS COUNCIL
ENGLAND**

INTERNATIONAL PLAYWRIGHTS AT THE ROYAL COURT

Since 1992 the Royal Court has placed a renewed emphasis on the development of international work and a creative dialogue now exists with theatre practitioners all over the world including Brazil, Cuba, France, Germany, India, Mexico, Nigeria, Palestine, Romania, Russia, Spain and Syria, and with writers from seven countries from the Near East and North Africa region. All of these development projects are supported by the Genesis Foundation and the British Council.

The Royal Court has produced new International plays through this programme since 1997, most recently The Stone by Marius von Mayenburg in February 2009 and Bliss by Olivier Choinière, translated by Caryl Churchill in Spring 2008. In 2007, the Royal Court presented a season of five new international plays – The Ugly One by Marius von Mayenburg (Germany), Kebab by Gianina Carbunariu (Romania), Free Outgoing by Anupama Chandrasekhar (India), and a double bill of The Good Family by Joakim Pirinen (Sweden) and The Khomenko Family Chronicles by Natalia Vorozhbit (Ukraine). Free Outgoing by Anupama Chandrasekhar and The Ugly One by Marius von Mayenburg transferred to the Jerwood Theatre Downstairs in Summer 2008 as part of the Upstairs-Downstairs season. Other recent work includes On Insomnia and Midnight by Edgar Chías (Mexico), My Name is Rachel Corrie, edited from the writings of Rachel Corrie by Alan Rickman and Katharine Viner, Way to Heaven by Juan Mayorga (Spain), Amid the Clouds by Amir Reza Koohestani (Iran), At the Table and Almost Nothing by Marcos Barbosa (Brazil), Plasticine, Black Milk and Ladybird by Vassily Sigarev (Russia), and Terrorism and Playing the Victim by the Presnyakov Brothers (Russia).

THE ROYAL COURT IN INDIA

Since 1996 eight emerging playwrights from India have been participants in the Royal Court International Residency which takes place for one month in London every summer, including Anupama Chandrasekhar who took part in this programme in 2000. This participation has been made possible with the support of the Charles Wallace India Trust.

In January 2001 the Royal Court ran a two week residency workshop for writers from all parts of India organised in collaboration with the British Council and the Artistes Repertory Theatre in Bangalore. The Royal Court team (Elyse Dodgson, Dominic Cooke and April de Angelis) also travelled to Mumbai, Pune and Delhi to investigate expanding the work. Following this, in November 2001, nine of the original playwrights worked with a group of directors on developing their plays with Ramin Gray and Hettie Macdonald. Seven of these plays were shown as part of a festival of new writing in Bangalore in October 2002.

Following the success of this project, Phyllida Lloyd and Carl Miller ran a second residency in Mumbai in September/October 2002 in collaboration with Rage Theatre. The follow-up of this work was led by the same team in September 2003. In April 2004 nine plays were fully produced as part of the first new writing Festival in Mumbai- Writers Bloc. In June 2005, the Royal Court invited four of the nine writers to work on new plays with us in London. In March 2006, Phyllida Lloyd and Carl Miller returned to Mumbai to work with a new group of writers from all parts of India again in collaboration with Rage Theatre. 11 of these plays were produced as part of the second Writers' Bloc Festival in Mumbai during January 2007.

In Spring 2010, the Royal Court will return to India to start a new project with emerging playwrights from all over India.

The Genesis Foundation supports the Royal Court's International Playwrights Programme. To find and develop the next generation of professional playwrights, Genesis funds workshops in diverse countries and residencies at the Royal Court. The Foundation's involvement extends to productions and rehearsed readings. Genesis helps the Royal Court offer a springboard for young writers to greater public and critical attention. For more information, please visit: www.genesisfoundation.org.uk.

DISCONNECT is presented as part of International Playwrights, A Genesis Foundation Project, and produced by the Royal Court's International Department:

Associate Director **Elyse Dodgson**
International Projects Manager **Chris James**
International Assistant **William Drew**

PROGRAMME SUPPORTERS

The Royal Court (English Stage Company Ltd) receives its principal funding from Arts Council England, London. It is also supported financially by a wide range of private companies, charitable and public bodies, and earns the remainder of its income from the box office and its own trading activities.

The Genesis Foundation supports the Royal Court's work with International Playwrights. The Jerwood Charitable Foundation supports new plays by new playwrights through the Jerwood New Playwrights series. Theatre Local is sponsored by Bloomberg.

The Artistic Director's Chair is supported by a lead grant from The Peter Jay Sharp Foundation, contributing to the activities of the Artistic Director's office. Over the past ten years the BBC has supported the Gerald Chapman Fund for directors.

ROYAL COURT DEVELOPMENT ADVOCATES
John Ayton
Elizabeth Bandeen
Tim Blythe
Anthony Burton
Sindy Caplan
Cas Donald (Vice Chair)
Allie Esiri
Celeste Fenichel
Anoushka Healy
Stephen Marquardt
Emma Marsh (Chair)
Mark Robinson
William Russell
Deborah Shaw Marquardt (Vice Chair)
Nick Wheeler
Daniel Winterfeldt

PUBLIC FUNDING
Arts Council England, London
British Council

CHARITABLE DONATIONS
American Friends of the Royal Court Theatre
Anthony Burton
Gerald Chapman Fund
Columbia Foundation
Credit Suisse First Boston Foundation*
Cowley Charitable Trust
The Edmond de Rothschild Foundation*
Do Well Foundation Ltd*
The D'Oyly Carte Charitable Trust
Frederick Loewe Foundation*
Genesis Foundation
The Goldsmiths' Company
Jerwood Charitable Foundation
John Thaw Foundation
John Lyon's Charity
The Laura Pels Foundation*
Marina Kleinwort Trust
The Martin Bowley Charitable Trust
The Andrew W. Mellon Foundation

The Patchwork Charitable Foundation*
Paul Hamlyn Foundation
Jerome Robbins Foundation*
Rose Foundation
Royal College of Psychiatrists
The Peter Jay Sharp Foundation*
Sobell Foundation

CORPORATE SUPPORTERS & SPONSORS
BBC
Bloomberg
Ecosse Films
Moët & Chandon

BUSINESS BENEFACTORS & MEMBERS
Grey London
Hugo Boss
Lazard
Merrill Lynch
Vanity Fair

AMERICAN FRIENDS OF THE ROYAL COURT
Rachel Bail
Francis Finlay
Amanda Foreman & Jonathan Barton
Imelda Liddiard
Stephen McGruder & Angeline Goreau
Alexandra Munroe & Robert Rosenkranz
Ben Rauch & Margaret Scott
David & Andrea Thurm
Amanda Vaill & Tom Stewart
Monica Voldstad
Franklin Wallis

INDIVIDUAL MEMBERS

ICE-BREAKERS
Act IV
Anonymous
Rosemary Alexander
Ossi & Paul Burger
Mrs Helena Butler
Lindsey Carlon
Virginia Finegold

Charlotte & Nick Fraser
The David Hyman Charitable Trust
David Lanch
Watcyn Lewis
David Marks QC
Nicola McFarland
Janet & Michael Orr
Pauline Pinder
Mr & Mrs William Poeton
Wendy Press
The Really Useful Group
Lois Sieff OBE
Gail Steele
Nick & Louise Steidl

GROUND-BREAKERS
Anonymous
Moira Andreae
Jane Attias*
Elizabeth & Adam Bandeen
Dr Kate Best
Philip Blackwell
Stan & Val Bond
Mrs D H Brett
Sindy & Jonathan Caplan
Mr & Mrs Gavin Casey
Tim & Caroline Clark
Kay Ellen Consolver
Clyde Cooper
Ian Cormack
Mr & Mrs Cross
Andrew & Amanda Cryer
Robyn M Durie
Denise Dumas
Allie Esiri
Edwin Fox Foundation
Celeste & Peter Fenichel
John Garfield
Lydia & Manfred Gorvy
Nick & Julie Gould
Lord & Lady Grabiner
Richard & Marcia Grand*
Reade & Elizabeth Griffith
Don & Sue Guiney
Douglas & Mary Hampson
Nicholas Josefowitz
David P Kaskel & Christopher A Teano
Peter & Maria Kellner*
Mrs Joan Kingsley & Mr Philip Kingsley
Mr & Mrs Pawel Kisielewski
Kathryn Ludlow

Emma Marsh
Barbara Minto
North Street Trust
Murray North
Gavin & Ann Neath
William Plapinger & Cassie Murray*
Mr & Mrs Tim Reid
Mark Robinson
Paul Robinson
Paul & Jill Ruddock
William & Hilary Russell
Sally & Anthony Salz
Jenny Sheridan
Anthony Simpson
Sheila Steinberg
Brian D. Smith
Samantha & Darren Smith
Carl & Martha Tack
Edgar & Judith Wallner
Nick & Chrissie Wheeler
Katherine & Michael Yates

BOUNDARY-BREAKERS
Katie Bradford
Tim Fosberry

MOVER-SHAKERS
Anonymous
John & Annoushka Ayton
Cas & Philip Donald
Duncan Matthews QC
The David & Elaine Potter Charitable Foundation
Ian & Carol Sellars
Jan & Michael Topham

HISTORY-MAKERS
Jack & Linda Keenan*
Miles Morland

MAJOR DONORS
Rob & Siri Cope
Daniel & Joanna Friel
Deborah & Stephen Marquardt
Lady Sainsbury of Turville
NoraLee & Jon Sedmak*
The Williams Charitable Trust

*Supporters of the American Friends of the Royal Court (AFRCT)

FOR THE ROYAL COURT

Royal Court Theatre, Sloane Square, London SW1W 8AS
Tel: 020 7565 5050 Fax: 020 7565 5001
info@royalcourttheatre.com, www.royalcourttheatre.com

Artistic Director **Dominic Cooke**
Deputy Artistic Director **Jeremy Herrin**
Associate Director **Sacha Wares**[*]
Artistic Associate **Emily McLaughlin***
Diversity Associate **Ola Animashawun***
Education Associate **Lynne Gagliano***
PA to the Artistic Director **Victoria Reilly**

Literary Manager **Ruth Little**
Senior Reader **Nicola Wass****
Literary Assistant **Marcelo Dos Santos**

Associate Director International **Elyse Dodgson**
International Projects Manager **Chris James**
International Assistant **William Drew**

Studio Administrator **Clare McQuillan**
Writers' Tutor **Leo Butler***

Casting Director **Amy Ball**
Casting Assistant **Lotte Hines**

Head of Production **Paul Handley**
JTU Production Manager **Tariq Rifaat**
Production Administrator **Sarah Davies**
Head of Lighting **Matt Drury**
Lighting Deputy **Stephen Andrews**
Lighting Assistants **Katie Pitt, Jack Williams**
Lighting Board Operator **Tom Lightbody**
Head of Stage **Steven Stickler**
Stage Deputy **Duncan Russell**
Stage Chargehand **Lee Crimmen**
Chargehand Carpenter **Richard Martin**
Head of Sound **David McSeveney**
Sound Deputy **Alex Caplen**
Head of Costume **Iona Kenrick**
Costume Deputy **Jackie Orton**
Wardrobe Assistant **Pam Anson**

Executive Director **Kate Horton**
Head of Finance & Administration **Helen Perryer**
Planning Administrator **Davina Shah**
Senior Finance & Administration Officer **Martin Wheeler**
Finance Officer **Rachel Harrison***
Finance & Administration Assistant **Tessa Rivers**

Head of Communications **Kym Bartlett**
Marketing Manager **Becky Wootton**
Press & Public Relations Officer **Anna Evans**
Communications Assistant **Ruth Hawkins**
Communications Intern **David Nock**
Sales Manager **Kevin West**
Deputy Sales Manager **Daniel Alicandro**
Box Office Sales Assistants **Cheryl Gallacher,
Ciara O'Toole**

Head of Development **Gaby Styles**
Senior Development Manager **Hannah Clifford**
Trusts & Foundations Manager **Khalila Hassouna**
Development Officer **Lucy Buxton**
Development Assistant **Penny Saward**
US Fundraising Counsel **Tim Runion**
Development Intern **Fred Kenny**

Theatre Manager **Bobbie Stokes**
Deputy Theatre Manager **Daniel O'Neill**
Front of House Manager **Siobhan Lightfoot**
Duty Managers **Stuart Grey***, **Claire Simpson***
Bar & Food Manager **Baljinder Kalirai**
Events Manager **Joanna Ostrom**
Assistant Bar & Food Manager **Sami Rifaat**
Head Chef **Charlie Brookman**
Bookshop Manager **Simon David**
Assistant Bookshop Manager **Edin Suljic***
Bookshop Assistant **Vanessa Hammick** *
Customer Service Assistant **Deidre Lennon***
Stage Door/Reception **Simon David***, **Paul Lovegrove,
Tyrone Lucas**

Thanks to all of our box office assistants, ushers and bar staff.

** The post of Senior Reader is supported by NoraLee & Jon Sedmak through the American Friends of the Royal Court Theatre.

* Part-time.

ENGLISH STAGE COMPANY

President
Dame Joan Plowright CBE

Honorary Council
Sir Richard Eyre CBE
Alan Grieve CBE
Martin Paisner CBE

Council
Chairman **Anthony Burton**
Vice Chairman **Graham Devlin CBE**

Members
Jennette Arnold
Judy Daish
Sir David Green KCMG
Joyce Hytner OBE .
Stephen Jeffreys
Wasfi Kani OBE
Phyllida Lloyd CBE
James Midgley
Sophie Okonedo
Alan Rickman
Anita Scott
Katharine Viner
Stewart Wood

Feb – August 2010

Jerwood Theatre Downstairs

11 February – 13 March

off the endz
By Bola Agbaje
Jerwood New Playwrights.
Supported by the Jerwood Charitable Foundation

9 April – 22 May

posh

By Laura Wade

11 June – 24 July

sucker punch
By Roy Williams
Tickets on-sale by 27 February

Jerwood Theatre Upstairs

31 March – 1 May

the empire
By DC Moore
Jerwood New Playwrights. Supported by the Jerwood Charitable Foundation

20 May – 19 June

ingredient x
By Nick Grosso

14 July – 14 August

spur of the moment
By Anya Reiss
Jerwood New Playwrights. Supported by the Jerwood Charitable Foundation

020 7565 5000 Tickets from £10
www.royalcourttheatre.com
Royal court Theatre, Sloane Square, London, SW1W 8AS

DISCONNECT

Anupama Chandrasekhar

Characters

AVINASH, *male, mid-forties, clearly Indian accent*
ROSS, *male, early twenties, American accent*
JYOTHI, *female, mid-twenties, fake American accent*
GIRI, *male, early twenties, neutral accent*
VIDYA, *female, early twenties, neutral accent*

None of the characters has been to America

Setting

The action takes place in Chennai, India

Notes

'BlitzTel' – *a call centre based in Chennai; handles inbound and outbound calls. Their major client is True Blue Capital, based in Buffalo, US*

'True Blue Capital' – *a finance company; offers Helium credit cards*

'Soup' – *supervisor*

'Mark' – *debtor*

A forward slash in the text (/) indicates the point at which the next speaker interrupts, or overlapping dialogue.

'Cacophony' refers to simultaneous dialogue where it's not clear what is being said.

'Beep' indicates that the person on the other end of the line has disconnected.

*Dialogue in [square brackets] is non-verbal communication –
either gestures or soundlessly mouthing the words.*

*In general, wherever there are simultaneous calls or dialogues,
the one on the left is audible.*

Acknowledgements

My debt to:

Indhu Rubasingham, Elyse Dodgson and her team, Dominic
Cooke, Ruth Little.

The night owls: Samit Kapoor, Jaspreet Kaur Chakkal, Iswar
Srikumar, Niranjana, David, Jai, Shyam.

Above all, my parents.

A.C.

*This text went to press before the end of rehearsals and so may
differ slightly from the play as performed.*

Scene One

JYOTHI*'s office.*

JYOTHI. Sorry. Like, I got held up at a a a. I had meetings non-
stop. I couldn't sneak away. Okay. I'm Jyothi, actually.
People call me Sharon. (*Laughs.*) I used to be Jennifer in
inbound and Michelle in outbound. But I always wanted to
be Kate. Like Winslet. Or Hudson.

AVINASH. Jyothi.

JYOTHI. Yeah. (*Looks in her folder.*) Avinash.

AVINASH. Yes.

JYOTHI. AKA...?

AVINASH. Just Avinash.

Pause.

JYOTHI. Right.

Pause.

AVINASH. You had purple hair before.

JYOTHI. Deep plum. Streaks, actually. In sunlight. Neon dis-
torts colour. God, you noticed that! It was many months ago.
God, it's stuffy here. Don't you think? I can't think in here.

AVINASH. Work is work, whatever the temperature.

Pause.

JYOTHI. Yeah, that's a good funda. (*Pause.*) Okay. Cool. Right.
This is... God, at times like this, I need a. I'm going to get
me a Coke. Shall I get you one too? I mean, do people like
you drink Coke, Avinash?

AVINASH. People like me drink coffee.

JYOTHI. Coffee. Yeah. Yeah. So do we, actually. Coffee.

Coffee. Cool. Steaming hot. God. This has been a mad crazy.

JYOTHI *places a styrofoam cup under the coffee machine and presses a button. They wait.*

They go, 'Can you find us some more collectors, you always do.' And I go, 'What am I? An employment agency?' And they go, 'You know people. You have friends everywhere, class-mates. Maybe a few will be interested.' And I go, 'Right. Half my class is already here. What more do you want from me?'

JYOTHI *laughs and hands* AVINASH *his coffee.*

AVINASH. Thank you.

JYOTHI *goes to another machine for her Coke.*

JYOTHI. You've been with us, what, four years now?

AVINASH. My history with the owners goes further back. Through another company. Have you heard of Blitz Publishers?

JYOTHI. Not / really.

AVINASH. It's defunct now. We published educational books. We brought out the Easy Speak English series. Fourteen years in all.

JYOTHI. Right. Flashback. So. Are you happy here? At BlizTel? Now?

AVINASH. I'm pleased.

JYOTHI. 'Pleased'?

AVINASH. Happy. Definitely.

JYOTHI. Happiness is the key. We discussed it at the, at the. Why?

AVINASH. Pardon?

JYOTHI. Why are you happy?

AVINASH. Because I have a window cubicle. (*Laughs. Pause.*) It's a joke.

JYOTHI. O-kay.

AVINASH. What's not to be happy here? I'm in the business of words. I like the team. They're a young bunch.

JYOTHI. Anyhoo. We need happy personnel so we can have happy customers. Right? That's why we have smileys everywhere. Still, our monthly collections are, like, depressing.

AVINASH. It's the times we are in.

JYOTHI. We are in this business because of the times. Bad times are good times, Avinash. That's the whole, like, point. The funda is, True Blue is closing down their New Jersey office in a few months. If we want them to, you know, offshore, we need to double our collections. Pronto. Because some stupid Filipino company is also keen. Bob let it out in, in, inadv –

AVINASH. – ertently.

JYOTHI. Yeah. So. This means underperformers must be, you know? (*Pause.*) The need of the hour is dynamism, energy and youth. (*Pause.*) Is the coffee very bad?

AVINASH. How old is young?

JYOTHI. Sorry?

AVINASH. Because you mentioned youth.

Pause.

JYOTHI. Well. The thing is. Here's your appraisal report. We've, like, rated all employees by A) their Aptitude, B) Attitude, C) Performance, and D) Commitment.

JYOTHI *gives the papers to* AVINASH.

As you will see on page fourteen, you fall under the underperforming-employee category… Non-achievement of weekly and monthly goals… low peer rating… low rating from team members.

AVINASH. Really? That's a – that's a surprise. Who scored me low?

JYOTHI. I can't say that. Sorry. (*Pause*.) Avinash. We don't think you're happy in New York –

AVINASH. What? No, I'm happy, I'm smiling, see?

JYOTHI. We've decided to. It's part of our core strategy to 1) Enthuse workers in a rut, 2) Caution non-performers, and 3) –

AVINASH. Are you enthusing me or cautioning me? (*Pause*.) Jyothi, there must be some mistake.

JYOTHI. That's so weird, you know? Every single person in your category says that. 'There must be a mistake.' You press a button, like for coffee or something, and out comes that line. Your team members were very, you know?

AVINASH. No, I don't know.

JYOTHI. Frank.

AVINASH. I'm the most committed person in this building.

JYOTHI. That's, wow –

AVINASH. You'll understand this when you're older, but a good supervisor is not necessarily loved by everyone. My team, the boys are very bright, but they're very young. It's my job to ensure that they they focus – that's what you pay me for. You're the good cop. Someone has to be the bad cop.

JYOTHI (*looks in her folder*). According to your peers, you've not been able to adapt to our culture, our lifestyle or our way of working. The management concludes this could be a problem.

AVINASH. It's my age, isn't it? That's the issue here.

JYOTHI. No, we value experience in in in –

AVINASH. I don't think you do. Because if you did, you'd see I've never taken leave, not medical, not casual. I've always been on time. All those things counted before.

JYOTHI. See page eleven? It says: 'Resistance to change; resistance to our core philosophy of dynamism.'

AVINASH. That's rubbish.

JYOTHI. Please, you're –

AVINASH. In my fourteen years –

JYOTHI. Four –

AVINASH. I've not jumped jobs. I've stayed put and slaved like a dog. Like a dog. That amounted to something in my days. You can't take arbitrary decisions on the basis of some moronic report cooked up by kids. You can't judge my competence based on half-baked information given by disgruntled juveniles. If you had my experience you'd know that.

JYOTHI. Please sit down, Avinash.

AVINASH. You youngsters come and go. But me, I'll be here long after you flit to the next company. I'm the pillar here.

JYOTHI. Unfortunately, your figures don't, like –

AVINASH. I'm not the only one who's got bad figures the last few months. Blame America. Blame the Americans. Don't blame me. You want figures, give me more voices, give me collectors with seriousness and focus.

JYOTHI. Don't yell at me. I'm actually trying to help you here.

You are not up to speed in this job, Avinash. That's, like, the issue here. New York is, you know, too fast for you. Not just speech-wise. We think you don't really have the aptitude.

AVINASH. 'Aptitude'? That's rubbish. I have high language skills. An earlier report said that.

JYOTHI. We can't take chances. Not when we'll be bidding. For the offshore, you know, after the 4th of July party. (*Pause.*) We value your loyalty, Avinash. We really do. That's why we're, like, trying to. Because, to be honest, there really is no place for you.

Silence.

AVINASH. If there's anything lacking in me, I'll – I'll learn. I'm a good learner.

Silence.

My daughter drinks Coke too. All that sugar and fizz... But she says she can study better after a bottle – She's in engineering.

Silence.

JYOTHI. Illinois. I can put you in Illinois. You'll be happy in Illinois. The delinquents there are more... civilised. Not like New York. And you have a supercollector in the team.

AVINASH. I know New York inside-out.

JYOTHI. Learn Illinois.

AVINASH. Let me stay on. I'll show you –

JYOTHI. God, everyone wants to be in New York! It's not a bunch of bananas for you to haggle over. You are showing definite resistance to change and our core values.

AVINASH. No, I'm sorry.

JYOTHI. It's either Illinois or. You are either with us or you can, like, you know, not work here.

So, what do you say?

Pause.

AVINASH. Where is Illinois?

JYOTHI. The Fourth Floor.

Scene Two

Illinois, the Fourth Floor.

ROSS (*into mic*). Good morning! I'd like to speak with –

VIDYA (*into mic*). If I may have a minute of your time –

GIRI (*into mic*). I see from our records –

ROSS. You missed payments –

VIDYA. For four –

GIRI. Five –

ROSS. Six months –

GIRI. You have an outstanding debt of –

VIDYA. Four thousand –

GIRI. Five hundred and –

VIDYA. Fifty-five dollars –

GIRI. Plus interest of –

ROSS. I know you are busy –

VIDYA. It won't take a min –

ROSS. I understand –

VIDYA. That's too bad but –

GIRI. When can we expect –

VIDYA. Direct bank transfer preferably –

ROSS. Or cheque –

VIDYA. If not the entire amount –

GIRI. How much can you pay –

ROSS. Please, Mr –

GIRI. Mrs –

VIDYA. Ms –

GIRI. If you'd just –

ROSS. I'm sorry to bother you but –

VIDYA. Please don't hang up. A minute –

GIRI. A minute is all I ask.

Beep.

No, ma'am. I'm not calling from India.

Ban-ga-lore? Where's that? (*Laughs.*)

ROSS *bowls a paper ball in* VIDYA*'s direction, trying to get her attention.* VIDYA *ignores it.*

VIDYA. According to our records, you haven't paid your out-standing dues for four months.

GIRI. Gary. G-A-R-Y E-V-A-N-S. Does my name sound Chinese to you?

ROSS *bowls another paper ball.* VIDYA *swats it away without turning in* ROSS*'s direction.*

VIDYA. I hope you find a good job. Coming back to your dues –

GIRI. My accent is the same as yours, ma'am.

VIDYA. I'm going to be honest with you, Mr James. Your credit score is scraping the bottom.

GIRI. I'm sorry, the manager is travelling. You simply have to –

VIDYA. Uh-huh.

She's not available either –

Uh-huh.

Kindly hold while I transfer your call to my supervisor.

Uh-huh.

Yes, ma'am. American.

I understand.

GIRI (*off mic*). I'm more American than you'll ever be, you
    ffffff –

VIDYA (*to* GIRI). Shhh. (*Into mic.*) That's terrible.

GIRI. Ross.

ROSS. What?

GIRI. Help. Escalation.

ROSS. Later.

GIRI. The mark won't wait.

ROSS. Busy, dude.

GIRI. It's only Facebook.

ROSS. It's research.

VIDYA. Unless you make a
    payment in full, I cannot
    help you.

I understand, I'm sorry.

GIRI (*to* VIDYA). [Will you take long?]

VIDYA *ignores* GIRI.

VIDYA. I – You're right, I don't believe you. Because I have
    the bills for your last few purchases.

GIRI. Fuck. (*To* ROSS.) Please, man. Everyone else is on call.

ROSS *bowls a paper ball into a trash bin.*

Fuck. (*To* VIDYA.) Please, someone. Anyone.

VIDYA. If you were so badly off, you had no business buying a
    big-screen plasma in February.

GIRI *kneels in front of* VIDYA.

How much – how much can you pay us right now? (*To*
GIRI.) [Ask him.]

GIRI *shakes his head, 'No'.*

ROSS. Hey.

VIDYA (*to* ROSS). Take over.

VIDYA *is about to continue with her call.*

GIRI. You heard her.

ROSS. If she asks me.

VIDYA. I did.

Beat.

GIRI. Just ask him.

VIDYA (*to* ROSS). Handle the call.

ROSS (*to* GIRI). If she asks me nicely –

GIRI. Ask nicely –

VIDYA. Handle the damn call, please.

GIRI. She said it nicely, she said 'please'. Hurry hurry.

ROSS *hasn't made a move.*

VIDYA (*into mic*). Here's what I can do for you.

GIRI. Fuck you. What do you want from me?

My iPod? My, my Rolex?

She's from Chicago.

VIDYA. May I suggest that you make a partial payment now, and the rest when you get your job?

ROSS. Your 3D Angelina Jolie or nothing.

Beat.

GIRI. Fine!

VIDYA. Of course, you can choose to roll over the –

GIRI (*louder*). I said fine.

VIDYA (*off mic*). [Shh.] (*Into mic.*) Or not pay at all. What do you think your chances are for getting that loan you've applied for with your credit history?

In the meantime, GIRI *has given* ROSS *the postcard-sized picture of Angelina Jolie in 3D.*

ROSS. What do you know, still on hold. White chick?

GIRI. No, cranky aunty.

ROSS. Me?

GIRI. Soup.

ROSS. Assistant manager.

GIRI. Just talk!

ROSS (*into mic, in heavy French accent*). Good morning, Mrs Schwartz.

GIRI. Aaah nooo.

VIDYA. Will you shut up?

ROSS. Zank you for being on hold. I apologise for any inconvenience.

VIDYA. Will you shut up? Oh, hell. Not you, sir, I mean – I'm sorry. That wasn't for you –

ROSS. Mrs Schwartz, I apologise for my colleague's rudeness – he's new.

VIDYA. No, sir, it's not a threat, I was merely... 'Hell' is not a profanity.

ROSS (*to GIRI, gleefully*). She hung up.

GIRI *tries to snatch the picture without disturbing* VIDYA *but it's not possible.* VIDYA *tries to separate* GIRI *and* ROSS.

VIDYA. Why don't I – call you back tomorrow when you've had time to process what I've said? Thank you and have a nice day.

GIRI. Look, it's his fault. All he had to do was speak fucking American. You back-stabber, you could have nailed her, but no, you have to torment me, vampire, bloodsucker, I'll kill you –

VIDYA (*into mic*). I told you to keep your voice down. There's people working.

GIRI. He could have converted. Bastard. Thank God it's the end of the week. Thank God, we don't have a soup yet – I mean, you're there. But not for long. That's not why I'm thanking God. I mean, if we get a new soup, I'd like it to be you.

VIDYA. Giri. Go take a break.

ROSS. Yeah, get us coffee or something.

What? He's the junior here. He's legally bound to serve us.

GIRI *tries to snatch the picture, fails.*

GIRI. Give me back my Angie. You've not earned her.

VIDYA. I'd like coffee. Has the machine been fixed?

GIRI. I don't know.

ROSS. So, go find out, will you?

VIDYA. Just go.

GIRI (*to* VIDYA). I want her back on my desk.

GIRI *leaves.*

VIDYA *turns away from* ROSS.

ROSS. My brother's visa interview took for ever and –

VIDYA (*into mic*). Hello, am I speaking with –

ROSS. I'm sorry, okay?

VIDYA (*off mic*). Call her back. (*Into mic.*) Is that Mrs Mandelsohn?

ROSS (*into mic*). Hello, Mrs Schwartz. I'm Ross Adams calling from True Blue's Buffalo office.

(*Laughs.*) I get that all the time! I apologise for any inconvenience caused by those Indian b – boys.

VIDYA. I'm calling about your Helium credit card. Your outstanding due is $16,289, including late fee and interest. How would you like to make a –

Ma'am. You are one of the cardholders. You are

(*Laughs.*)

Born and raised in Chicago, ma'am. Edgewater.

It's a small world. I lived two blocks away. On Acorn Street.

Right. Coming to your card, you'd reported it missing or stolen last –

No no no don't cry, Beth –

as liable to pay as –

Ma'am –

Ma'am, please –

How may I get hold of him?

Does he have a contact –

Ma'am, which hotel is he staying in in the Samoan Islands –

Beep.

GIRI *is at the coffee machine. He presses a button.*

ROSS *sees that* VIDYA *is done with her call.*

ROSS (*off mic*). So. Good movie? (*Into mic.*) May I call you Beth?

GIRI *bangs his fist against the machine. Water, not coffee, pours into the styrofoam cup.*

VIDYA. Yes.

ROSS. So, you did watch –

VIDYA. Oh, yeah. With Giri. He was free. (*Into mic.*) Hi. Is Mr Mandelsohn in –

GIRI *pours water into the pots of dried cacti on the supervisor's desk.* GIRI *exits.*

ROSS (*into mic*). Beth, Beth. It's okay if you lose a card.

You found it? I don't under –

I know you're not a bad person.

VIDYA. When is he likely to be –

I gather it's a working –

It is a very urgent matter. I'm afraid I can only discuss with him.

His wife said you'd have

Tell me, what's the matter?

Who is leaving you?

He sounds like a rat.

Let the rat pack his bags. You are made of strong stuff.

I know because it's in your voice.

Voice can reveal character.

Where did you work before, Beth?

I'm sure they'd love to have you back.

Why don't I e-mail you some links to job sites right now?

Just hold on a sec.

There we are. Check your inbox.

his hotel details –

A phone number, his hotel number –

I can't reveal that, ma'am. It's a confidential matter.

It's very very important that I speak with him.

Monday, when he returns and finds out I've not been able to contact him all week, he's going to be very very angry.

We all know how angry he can get.

Pause.

I'm Vicki Lewis. Thank you very much. Have a great day.

Beep.

ROSS (*off mic, to* VIDYA). Look, I'm really –

VIDYA (*to* ROSS). Your numbers are down this week.

ROSS. It's still higher than anyone else's in Illinois.

VIDYA. People can catch up. Giri can catch up.

Beat.

ROSS (*into mic*). Got it? Great.

I want you to know, you're not alone. Okay?

First things first. You have an outstanding balance of $2,800. How much can you pay?

That bad, huh?

Wait a minute, Beth.

Do you know where he keeps his credit cards?

Do you know where his wallet is?

(*Off mic*.) They've found a new soup.

VIDYA. Sorry?

ROSS. Your replacement.

ROSS (*into mic*). Yes, Beth, did you find his card?

A statement, great! What does it say?

It means, he is a piece of work. He pays his bills, his girlfriend's bills, but not his wife's.

Do you realise you have power in your hands?

Silence.

I can't tell you.

I can't tell you what to do.

Silence.

(*Smiles*.) Good girl. As you requested, I'm going to make a quick transaction for $2,800. May I have the card number now?

And the expiry date?

VIDYA (*into mic*). Hi, is this the Bay Jewel Resort?

Is there a Mandelsohn staying with you?

Great. Can you please connect me to him?

But it's a very important matter. I must speak to him immediately.

Thank you very much.

Pause.

Hello, Mr Mandelsohn. I'm sorry to disturb you. I'm Vicki Lewis. Your Helium credit card dues are –

Your wife said you'd pay up.

No, no, she said to ask you.

She will not –

Mr Mandelsohn. Your dues amount to –

ROSS. It's through, Beth. Congratulations. You can start your new, single life with a clean credit. I always say: Americans got to stick up for Americans because no one else in the world is going to. Have a nice day!

(*Off mic*.) $2,800, babe. Payment in full. Giri can't catch up now and Angie is mine for ever.

Pause.

You don't actually like being a supervisor, do you?

VIDYA. No no. It was getting tiresome – the responsibility and the collecting.

ROSS. Do you want to know who the new guy is?

ROSS *clicks*. AVINASH*'s picture looms up on the computer screen*.

VIDYA. He looks familiar. (*Pause*.) He's that guy from the canteen. The weirdo who kept staring at me when I finished up your bottle of Bacardi. Remember?

ROSS. My dad has a shirt just like that.

VIDYA. Hell. He's older than my dad.

ROSS. Uncle's name is Avinash.

VIDYA. How did you get that?

ROSS. Where's my cellphone?

VIDYA. I checked the blog and Twitter just five minutes ago.

ROSS. Oh, there it is.

VIDYA. Oh, Ross.

ROSS. It's nothing.

VIDYA. Ross. You promised.

ROSS. It's not a crime.

GIRI (*off*). Are you looking for someone?

VIDYA. Really? Hacking into confidential files?

AVINASH (*off*). A coffee machine first.

ROSS. It's not a big deal. No harm done.

GIRI (*off*). That's in there. Damn, you're fast. I spoke to your boss five minutes ago.

AVINASH enters. GIRI follows him with a cellphone in his hand. ROSS closes the page on the computer but AVINASH has already seen his picture on it.

AVINASH (*to* ROSS). Is this Illinois?

ROSS. Do you want it to be?

VIDYA. This is Illinois.

GIRI. So. Where are your tools?

AVINASH. 'Tools'?

VIDYA. Giri, you don't –

AVINASH. Do you mean the employment manual?

GIRI. Um. Don't you have a screwdriver or something?

AVINASH. No.

VIDYA. Giri, he's the...

VIDYA shuts up.

GIRI. What do you start work with?

AVINASH. Always, with some coffee.

GIRI (*laughs*). That's a good one. Get on with it. We haven't got all night.

AVINASH. I'm Avinash. I'm your new supervisor.

GIRI. Oh. (*Pause.*) Welcome!

Silence from the other two.

Where were you working before?

AVINASH. Here.

GIRI *puts his cellphone in his shirt pocket.*

GIRI. Oh. Right. Happens. You work in a place for years, you come and go every day but your paths never cross. You never meet the others, because you never take a break the same time as the others, because you are too preoccupied about customers and targets to notice the others. (*Laughs.*) That's your desk. It's a bit of a mess now because one of our earlier soups was botanically inclined. Feel free to dump them all in the bin.

AVINASH. No windows here.

GIRI. You aren't particular, are you? You won't find any on this floor.

That's why we call it the 'upstairs dungeon'. If you desperately need a window, there's a big sealed one by the stairs. It has a scenic view of the garbage dump. And, oh. The coffee machine doesn't work. But they're sending someone – someone who is not you. (*Laughs.*)

AVINASH. Thanks –

GIRI. Giri. Or Gary.

AVINASH. You're all aware paper is not allowed inside.

ROSS. It's a magazine.

AVINASH. This is an office, not a school dormitory. You know you are required to stay in your seats during the duration of the calls. I expect you not to dance about when you're working. (*To* GIRI.) As per the employee's manual, you're also required to leave your mobile phones in your lockers.

Pause.

Today, you may leave them on this table. You may collect them after work from the security.

Pause.

I don't have all night.

GIRI. Aw, man!

VIDYA *places her cellphone on the table.* AVINASH *looks at* GIRI. GIRI *pulls out all his things from a trouser pocket – a designer wallet, a funky gold keychain with a couple of keys – and displays them to* AVINASH *and replaces them in his pocket. From another pocket, a breath freshener. From yet another pocket, a cigarette case and lighter. Pause.* GIRI *takes out his cellphone and earphones from another pocket.* AVINASH *looks pointedly at* GIRI*'s shirt pocket. A long pause.* GIRI *reluctantly pulls out the cellphone.*

It's a BlackBerry Storm.

GIRI *puts all the items back in his pockets, except the phones.*

Take care of it, man. It cost me a bomb.

AVINASH *looks at* ROSS. ROSS *takes out his cellphone, deletes all messages.*

AVINASH. You needn't delete on my account. I won't be reading them, if that's what's worrying you.

ROSS *finishes deleting and places the phone on the table.*

Where are you off to? I'm not done yet.

ROSS. It will have to wait. I'm taking a loo break. That's allowed, according to the manual.

Scene Three

AVINASH*'s desk.* ROSS*'s voice emerges from the computer speakers. It's pure gibberish.*

MALE VOICE. I don't understand what you just said.

ROSS'S VOICE. Listen to me carefully. What I'm saying is – (*He speaks more gibberish.*)

MALE VOICE. I don't understand.

ROSS'S VOICE. Darn it! Do I have to repeat it all over again?

AVINASH. What is the meaning of this?

ROSS. Didn't you get it either?

Pause.

AVINASH. Do you think this is funny?

ROSS *shrugs*.

Do you ever stop to think you are part of something historic? What you do is of utmost importance to the world economy. You can help the call-centre industry grow. You can help an American finance company stay afloat. By saving True Blue, you may be saving America. If America is robust, India is robust, the world is robust. But you don't seem to understand the significance of your role. I don't get that sense at all.

ROSS. Dude, it's no big deal. At the end of it, he laughed.

AVINASH. Mr Harry Coltrane can sue us.

ROSS. For what? He needed to feel good. I made him feel good. End of matter.

AVINASH. How much has he paid so far?

ROSS. Look. He has four kids and / no money.

AVINASH. Nothing. He's spent $38,000 of our money –

ROSS. On the family, on the kids. We should have written off his case months ago.

AVINASH. That decision will be made by Bob's team.

ROSS. I send the file to them and they send it back to us. It's stupid and tiresome. I'm not going to get a cent off the guy. But since I have to go through the routine, I call him up every two weeks. We have a bit of fun. That's all.

AVINASH. Bob is not paying us to have fun or feel sorry. Bob is paying us to collect. And if Bob sends us a file back, it means Bob wants us to pursue the case.

ROSS. Harry has nothing left to give.

AVINASH. That's not our worry. We chase him till he pays up or files for bankruptcy or Bob changes his mind. Got that? No more games, Roshan –

ROSS. Ross –

AVINASH. Ross. Recessionary America is a brand-new battleground. Understand?

The phone rings. AVINASH *picks it up.*

Hello?

Who?

Just a moment.

AVINASH *hands* ROSS *the receiver.*

ROSS. For me?

Hello? Ross here.

Ma?

ROSS *turns away from* AVINASH. *He lowers his voice.*

I told you not to call me at work.

Yes, Ma. Fine!

I said I'd follow it up with the consulate, didn't I?

Bye.

ROSS *replaces the receiver and realises* AVINASH *has been busy watering the cacti.*

AVINASH. What kind of an attitude is that?

ROSS. Excuse me?

AVINASH. It's rude to use that accent on family.

ROSS (*snaps*). It's fucking ruder to eavesdrop.

Pause.

AVINASH. Listen, Roshan. Ross. We must be able to work together. We need to fare better as a team. We need to trust each other. I need to trust you to do your job and you need to trust me to do mine. Can we agree on that? On trusting each other? (*Pause*.) In the interest of the team.

Pause.

ROSS. Sure.

AVINASH. Good. (*Re: cacti*.) Do you know if the previous supervisor gave them anything apart from water?

ROSS. No.

Pause.

AVINASH. I want you to be honest with me.

ROSS. Sure.

AVINASH. The new targets –

ROSS. – are unreasonable and greedy.

AVINASH. Well. You don't know your own potential.

ROSS. Half a million dollars from Illinois in three months is insane. And you certainly can't expect $125,00 from fourth-stagers, man. Our marks are tough nuts. If they've not cracked with the early-stagers, what are the chances they'd crack with us? It's recession time, man.

AVINASH. I thank you to not use the R-word any more. Roshan. Ross. Listen. Fact is, you are the linchpin of the team. A supercollector. It's time you start taking a leader-ship role. Yes, guide the other ten collectors, bear the burden of –

ROSS. Dude. I don't bear burdens. Look. It's been a long night. The taxi's waiting.

AVINASH (*laughs*). What's five minutes when you've wasted seventeen doing your gibberish act? I think the targets are a piece of cake. If you focus and not get distracted. Your breaks are far too long. Half an hour is the allowed time for dinner, and two five-minute breaks. We've agreed –

ROSS. Are you serious? You want us to aim for $125,000 with just a half hour for dinner? No no no –

AVINASH. You're wasting a lot of time –

ROSS. I need to waste my time. That's my reset mode. I can't make call after call just like that. Collection is a fucking dementor of a job. Don't make it worse.

AVINASH *gives* ROSS *a spiral-bound book.*

AVINASH. You'll find your target easier to achieve if you use this.

Pause.

We said we'd trust each other. I believe going back to the script will speed up collection. Get more payments in full. Let's try my way for a couple of months and see if it works, huh?

ROSS. You may be right.

AVINASH. You agree?

ROSS. Focus. No distraction.

AVINASH. Yes.

ROSS. Just follow the script.

AVINASH. So you understand?

ROSS. Work, work, work.

AVINASH. Yes.

ROSS. Don't eat, drink or piss.

AVINASH. That's not –

ROSS. We talk non-stop for eight hours every night. Our mouths get parched, our throats dry up. We need to drink buckets of fluids to survive, but guess what, the coffee

machine has conked out. We got to fucking trek to the fifth
floor to get a fucking cup of coffee. That's how it is here.
Yeah, so we use the loo often, but is there a statutory restric-
tion on how many times you take a piss? Know something
else? Your cacti here get to drink more water than any of us.
How long did you collect?

AVINASH. Excuse me?

ROSS. You are a soup now. You've been here four years. How
long were you on fourth-stage collections?

AVINASH. What's that –

ROSS. How many months or years? Shall I tell you? Four
months. And did you reach your target? Come on, tell me.
Did you ever reach your target? Only twice. Twice in four
months. With an accent like that, no wonder they took you
off the hot seat.

AVINASH. You will not speak in any language but American
with the marks. You will not hang up on them without their
consent. You will not decide on a waiver arbitrarily. You will
run the debtor-assessment software every time, and only
upon its recommendations will you offer a waiver. Yes. You
will follow the script. Any deviation from the script will be
dealt with strictly.

Pause.

ROSS. You want me to be boring.

Pause.

AVINASH. Yes, exactly. Do your duty. That's what I say and
that's what the Gita says. Any drop in the daily figure for
seven consecutive days, you'll be stripped of your position
as supercollector. Oh, did I mention no blogs and Twitter?
No more social networking on office computers. All you'll
be allowed to use are the search engines. Do you understand? I'm taking you off the Harry Coltrane case.

Pause.

And Roshan. Please don't use dirty language in this office. Any questions?

ROSS. How can I have any questions when I'm not allowed to think in this ffff – felicitous office?

Scene Four

ROSS (*into mic*).	VIDYA (*into mic*).	GIRI (*into mic*).
Hi. This is Ross Adams of True Blue Capital. I've discussed your financial problems with my boss and I'm happy to say we have an offer you can't refuse. We are willing to waive your late charge and interest. This is a limited period offer only. For more details, please call 1-800-8687 immediately and ask for Ross. That's 1-800-U-O-US. This offer will expire on Wednesday the 15th April at 5 p.m. Please note, the offer	Hi. This is Vicki Lewis of True Blue Capital. I've discussed your financial problems with my boss and I'm happy to say we have an offer you can't refuse. We are willing to waive your late charge and interest. This is a limited period offer only. For more details, please call 1-800-8687 immediately and ask for Vicki. That's 1-800-U-O-US. This offer will expire on Wednesday the 15th April at 5 p.m. Please note, the offer	Hi. This is Gary Evans of True Blue Capital. I've discussed your financial problems with my boss and I'm happy to say we have an offer you can't refuse. We are willing to waive your late charge and interest. This is a limited period offer only. For more details, please call 1-800-8687 immediately and ask for Gary. That's 1-800-U-O-US. This offer will expire on Wednesday the 15th April at 5 p.m. Please note, the offer

| will expire on 15th April at 5 p.m. Thank you and have a great day. | will expire on 15th April at 5 p.m. Thank you and have a great day. | will expire on 15th April at 5 p.m. Thank you and have a great day. |

Silence.

ROSS, GIRI *and* VIDYA *have their headsets on.* GIRI *massages his cheeks, jaw.*

GIRI. I hate fucking Mondays.

VIDYA. Me too.

GIRI. And Fridays.

VIDYA. Me too. (*Laughs.*) My tongue is filing for a divorce from my mouth. I locked myself in my room yesterday, you know? I plugged my ears with cotton. Didn't speak a word. Parents thought I was sulking from last week's fight. They've no idea it was a brand-new sulk.

GIRI *flexes his jaw.*

GIRI. I need my caffeine fix now. What about you guys?

VIDYA. I'm good, thanks.

GIRI *exits.*

(*To* ROSS.) I wanted to call you on the weekend so we could meet and chill, but just the thought of one more phone call…

We must – hell. (*Into mic.*) Hi. May I speak with Harry Coltrane?

ROSS *turns his head sharply.*

Mrs Coltrane. It's very important –

The reason I called is your husband's payments, Mrs Coltrane. It's not my fault he's drowning in debt. (*Off mic.*) What's the matter?

ROSS *turns away.*

ROSS (*into mic*). Hi, I'm looking for Sara Johnson.

Ma'am –

Ma'am. What have I done?

I'm sorry I distracted you. How does your cake look?

Dark brown is not burnt. What were you baking?

Have you sprinkled nutmeg? Learnt it from my mother. Would you know how I can get in touch with Sara?

Which library might that be?

Springfield? Oh, she's moved again.

That's very very helpful. Thank you very much.

VIDYA *is perplexed. She watches him before she speaks into her mic.*

VIDYA (*into mic*). Hello –

No no, don't hang up!

I love *Desperate House-wives* too. Dave – my husband – and I try to watch –

The reason I called is, your Helium card payments are long overdue and –

Ma'am, this will only take a few seconds –

Or or I'll call you after the –

Beep.

– show. (*Pause.*) Bitch.

Pause.

VIDYA (*off mic*). Is it about Harry Coltrane? (*Pause.*) I'm sorry. Uncle said handle the case.

ROSS. Harry is depressed. He needs funny.

VIDYA. I don't do funny.

ROSS. Yeah. Funny is not in the script. (*Into mic.*) Is this the Springfield Public Library?

ROSS. I'd rather be helped by Ms Sara Johnson.

VIDYA (*into mic*). Is Mr Parker in?

No, not a date, of course not. Why? Is she hot?

It wouldn't be possible, bro, even if I wanted. I live in Buffalo.

A jet. Now, why didn't I think of it? And a mansion in Beverly Hills –

I dream big.

A BMW? Sweet. I lean towards the Merc myself.

Yeah, bro. Cool.

Camping. How wonderful for him.

The weather's gorgeous in in…

I love Mesa Verde. You can feel the history the moment you step foot on on on – the place. Yes, the mesa – How long is he camping?

May I have his cell number, please?

I wouldn't ask if it wasn't urgent.

I'll call back. Thank you.

VIDYA (*off mic, looking at* GIRI*'s figure on the whiteboard*). Giri's on a roll, isn't he?

ROSS (*off mic*). That means fuck-all if you got to read words off of a book every time to nail a mark. Where's the ability there? Fuck the script.

ROSS *waits to be transferred.*

The librarian sounds like he's a bouncer and the hold tune is Beethoven's Fifth. Who'll go to libraries that play Beethoven and hire bouncers?

Pause.

ROSS (*into mic*). Hi, is that Sara Johnson?

Pause.

It's been a long, long chase, Ms Johnson. Finally, after all these weeks, I find you.

VIDYA (*into mic*). It now amounts to $4,700 including late charges.

That was a year ago. If you'd paid up then, you'd have saved – let me see – nearly $2,000.

Congratulations on your new job at the Springfield Public Library. Let's talk about the dues on your Helium credit card.

So, when can you talk?

Not tomorrow, not next week. Now.

May I have your number, please?

That number no longer works.

I could do this again. I could call you at work. Would you prefer that?

That's more like it.

I'll call back in five minutes.

But it's not too late, Mr Casey.

How would you like to make a payment?

You have two options. You can make a minimum payment and roll over the rest to the next month.

You've done it before, I know. But I wouldn't advise it.

Uh-huh.

Uh-huh.

Rolls her eyes.

VIDYA (*off mic*). Did your brother get his visa?

ROSS. He got it. My parents think, after he finishes grad school, he'll get a job with Intel or Microsoft. (*Laughs.*) Like they have jobs there for us. (*Pause.*) You know where Rajan's headed? Chicago. He chose it over Boston because – get this – he felt as if his brother was there. What a geek. This is as good as America.

VIDYA (*into mic*). That's all well, Mr Casey. Being a good artist doesn't release you from your debt.

VIDYA *makes a face.*

(*To* ROSS.) [Spaced-out character.]

ROSS. [Hang up.]

VIDYA. [What?]

ROSS. Let's – let's head off to – the canteen. Or our window.

VIDYA. [I'm working here.]

ROSS. Fine – Let's – imagine we're going somewhere.

VIDYA (*off mic*). What?

ROSS. Close your eyes.

VIDYA. [Please –]

ROSS. Just one second. Close your –

VIDYA *closes her eyes.* VIDYA *opens her eyes.*

VIDYA (*into mic*). I'm not supposed to reveal this, Mr Casey – Simon. But what the heck.

Do you know what our biggest secret is? It actually makes economical sense to pay up on time.

Really.

Let's do the math. Do you have a pen and paper or a calculator? Why don't you go and fetch it?

ROSS (*into mic*). Marlon, hi, this is Ross Adams.

Are you having a good day, Marlon?

Uh-huh.

Did you have a chance to consider my offer?

You are running out of time.

I'm sorry, tomorrow will be too late.

ROSS (*off mic*). So where have you taken me?

VIDYA (*off mic*). Sorry?

ROSS. Where is this magical place?

VIDYA. I'm busy here –

ROSS. Humour me.

VIDYA. I don't know – (*Into mic.*) Hello, Simon? Paper to write on, Simon. You're an artist. You should have paper.

Pause.

ROSS. Right. I'll take you – to Sears Tower –

VIDYA. Willis Tower.

ROSS. It will always be Sears. We're on on the Skydeck, the ledge. It's a beautiful summer's day. The sun is –

VIDYA (*into mic*). Toilet paper will do just fine. Look at all the items you've bought so far. Acrylics. Brushes. Canvases. Add up all your bills.	ROSS (*into mic*). I've already waived $500. I can't go any further. Marlon, listen – Marlon. You've got a big family to take care of. You must set your house in order now, when you can.

ROSS (*off mic*). The sun shining bright. Clear blue skies. No sign of a –

VIDYA. How much does it come to?

ROSS. No people at all. Just us, on the glass ledge, open to the skies and the ground. It's like standing on air. The world –

ROSS (*into mic*). Your troubles won't vanish simply because you choose to ignore it. Fine. I'll call again tomorrow, but remember the offer is valid only till 5 p.m. CST today. (*Sighs*.) Have a great day, Marlon.	VIDYA. What is your result? What did you get when you subtracted – Yes, $4,000. You've paid $1,500 so far.

ROSS (*off mic*). The world under our feet. The sun on our faces, the air –

VIDYA (*off mic*). It would be terrifying to be that high up.

ROSS. I'm there. Nothing to be scared of.

Pause. A moment of connection.

VIDYA. Are we like on a date?

Pause.

ROSS. The city's spread before us, under us, like carpet. Little matchbox buildings –

GIRI *enters.*

VIDYA. We – we could imagine it. We could imagine being on a…

GIRI. On a what?

Pause.

VIDYA (*laughs*). We're living in Chicago.

GIRI. I'd live on a yacht.

GIRI *puts on his headset.*

Hi. This is Gary Evans.

VIDYA. Are we still on Sears?	GIRI. We spoke yesterday about your Helium balance. Have you mailed us the cheque for $1,250?
Pause.	
ROSS. Yeah.	Francine?
VIDYA. I think it'll be dead silent up there. I'd love to be there for ever. Just… us.	Why not?

Pause. VIDYA wheels her chair closer to ROSS. A moment.

ROSS (*into mic*). Hello, Sara, it's Ross here from	VIDYA. If you add up the late charges, you owe us $3,200 more. Think about this.

True Blue. I told you I'd call in five minutes.

Your outstanding balance on your Helium –

That was two months ago. Now it's $23,023.

I know that.

Well, you buy birdseeds. In my experience, birdseed buyers are difficult to get hold of, but yeah, they pay off their debt.

All of them so far. Seventeen.

Thank you – you have a lovely voice as well. Do you sing?

In a band?

You're in fact paying $4,700 for stuff that's worth only $4,000. You are paying $700 more for being late. And more if you don't clear your dues today.

Well, you could pay $250 and continue to roll over the debt to the next month, but that won't solve your problem.

Are you there?

For you, I'll knock off $200. You'll only have to write us a cheque for $3,000.

Everybody in America is going through this.

Let me make you a good deal. I'll knock off another $300. Pay us $2,700, and I'll consider

GIRI. Uh-huh.

Uh-huh.

No, we're going to sort this out now. You must make some sort of a payment today.

You signed a contract, Francine. You agreed to the terms, to the interest rate.

Well, yes, the rates would be high. You have no credit history, Francine. In this country, we need a credit history for everything.

I understand all that. Don't you want a green

Pink Hearts Club? It sounds like a girl band.

Oh, it is?

Well, yeah, I do too. There's three of us – we call ourselves Indebted. (*Laughs*.) No, not quite Backstreet Boys – it's – we're different. We do only vocals. Pure vocals. No instrument at all. We have fun.

Anyway, coming to your –

(*Laughs*.) No, Ms Johnson – Sara, debt never goes away. It's like a pesky little insect, it keeps circling you.

A bee, exactly. (*Laughs*.)

Sara, you need to look into your finances. Your credit score is in

all outstanding dues cleared. It's a one-off offer.

It's a great deal.

I can't go any lower than that and I can't make that offer again tomorrow. You got to decide now.

Why don't you do the math again, Simon?

Uh-huh.

Uh-huh.

I'm still here.

Where will I go?

card?

Will you get a green card when you're neck-deep in debt?

It does matter. Because when you applied for our card, you signed to our terms.

That's right. Please take a look at the agreement.

What does it say?

Read section 8b.

Did you find it?

This means, it doesn't matter if you're an American or not. You still have to pay up.

Well, you could, hypothetically fly back to France and leave behind your debt in America.

No, no, no, it will mean that

the red.

Don't worry. We'll figure this out, Sara. You've got a job now – that's good news. We'll take it step by step, okay?

I'm here to help you.

That's the spirit.

I'll call again in a few days with a plan of action.

Have a great day, Sara.

the moment you set foot on America, we'll know. We'll call you. Or, worse, send our representatives in person to collect. Now is not the right time for you to default, is it, Francine? Not when you're planning to stay on here.

ROSS *smiles*.

VIDYA (*off mic*). What? Nailed?

ROSS (*off mic*). No. Not yet.

Pause.

VIDYA. Ross, this is… It's nice to be like this…

GIRI. I'll call at six.

Pause.

VIDYA. We must…

ROSS. Yeah.

VIDYA *takes* ROSS*'s hand and places it against her cheek*.

GIRI. Bull's-eye. I got a Promise to Pay.

ROSS *pulls back his hand*. GIRI *goes to the whiteboard to enter his amount. '$1,250' under 'Promise to Pay'*.

Oh, before I forget...

GIRI *pulls out a money jar. On it is written: 'I love to party.'*

Team, be generous, cos Giri is gonna teach BlitzTel how to party.

(*To* VIDYA.) What? I do know a thing or two about galas. No samosas and pooris. It's gonna be hot dogs and hamburgers.

Pause. ROSS *hands him three hundred rupees.* VIDYA *ignores him.*

Look. I could sneak in vegetarian hamburgers for you – but that's the only concession I can make.

VIDYA *gives him money.*

Do you suppose they party these days, the Americans? I mean, if they don't have money and can't use cards and don't have anything to party for... what do you suppose they do on Fridays?

Scene Five

Cacophonic sounds of collection calls. The sounds die down to reveal:

ROSS (*laughs*). Well, that's a difficult one.

I'm six feet tall. Blond, blue-green eyes, medium build. Some day I'll own a Merc. But for now I drive a Ford. Black. I'm boring, sorry.

Well, how do I sound then?

(*Laughs.*) What do you mean, 'Like chocolate'? You got to be specific here. Do you mean I sound milky or bitter or dark? (*Laughs.*)

Yeah. (*He sings the* Friends *theme song.*) Nice harmony!

I'm single. Well, I was in a relationship for a while but we split up. We – we never really connected. (*Pause*.) How about you?

The man was a moron.

He wasn't much of a man either, was he?

Well, because you bought him the Viagra.

I have copies of all your bills, don't I?

I've been thinking about your finances. You're really in bad shape. But listen, I've a plan in place.

All you have to do is pay this month the minimum fee of $125. Next month you can –

You can. You must. With your poor credit record, the interest rate will keep going up. You can't get loans, you can't get another card. Do you understand?

You've got to take control of your life and your finances, Sara. Don't you want a home of your own? You've got to start saving up.

Oh, yeah?

A piggy bank?

Oh, my mom does that too – she's got a yellow sugar-bowl where she hides a small fortune. (*Laughs*.) I bet there's quite a bit in there.

Can you find out how much tonight?

I'll call again, same time tomorrow. We're going to do this, Sara. We're going to set your house in order together. Okay?

Thank you for your time, Sara. Have a wonderful day!

Scene Six

Sealed window. ROSS *sneaks in. He is relieved to see there's no one about.* ROSS *is about to take out his cellphone when* AVINASH *enters.*

AVINASH. There you are.

A moment of panic.

ROSS. Avinash, hi – What are you doing here?

AVINASH. So, this is the window.

ROSS. Yeah. But there's nothing to see here. If you want a view you could try the management section. They have two windows facing the highway.

AVINASH. Good thing it's nailed shut or the stench would send us to our graves. Do you know two thousand tonnes of garbage are dumped right here every night? People want their houses clean, so they dump their rubbish outside the city. But they forget, the city grows too. And now, the only way it can grow is through that pile of rubbish. (*Pause.*) I'm sometimes happy we work at night or everywhere we turn we'd see only the litter.

ROSS. Yeah. Yeah.

AVINASH. How's the collection today?

ROSS. Fine.

AVINASH. It means absolutely nothing these days, do you realise? Overuse of a word simply erodes the meaning.

ROSS. 'Fine' means, 'it will get better'. It's one of those days.

AVINASH. We have half a million dollars hanging in the balance, Roshan.

ROSS. There are ten others on the team. I don't see you get on their case.

AVINASH. They've not been as distracted as you the last few days.

ROSS. That's not true.

AVINASH. You've been very lax with the calls, lax with the time –

ROSS. I'm just trying to get them to trust me –

AVINASH. Focus on the money, Roshan. And keep an eye on the clock.

ROSS. Fine!

Pause.

AVINASH. And you must wear something more appropriate to work.

ROSS. Chill. When I'm working, I sound like I wear a suit.

Pause.

AVINASH. Have you always been a night owl, Roshan?

ROSS. What?

AVINASH. I was a morning bird. Sleeping late used to give me an acidic stomach. Now look at me, staying up all night. (*Laughs.*) My wife has a day job. I have a night job. I go to bed when she wakes up. I leave for work when she returns home. We e-mail each other every day. Sometimes we stick Post-it notes on the bedpost. She puts her notes on my side of the bed and I stick mine on her side.

ROSS. O-kay.

AVINASH. Sometimes I think we deserve better than this… place. We are nothing here. We are scavengers, cleaning up other people's mess.

Pause.

Is your brother ready for his trip?

ROSS. Nearly.

AVINASH. You're next in line for the visa, eh?

ROSS. No! Why would I want that?

AVINASH. I thought –

ROSS. You thought wrong.

AVINASH. It's not the end of the world to have one's visa application rejected a few times. You shouldn't take it to heart.

Pause.

ROSS. How do you know that?

AVINASH. You must have had a big culture shock when you arrived here. Tanjore is poles apart from Chennai. Believe me, I know.

ROSS. What are you talking about?

AVINASH. Your father said you're funding your brother's education. That's a very laudable thing to do, very old world – Your father is very proud of you.

ROSS. He called here?

AVINASH. No, I called him.

ROSS. Why?

AVINASH. As your boss, it's my duty to know my underlings –

ROSS. You have no business to poke your nose in my affairs. My private matters are private. Okay?

AVINASH. I felt proud when my boss came to visit me. Your parents felt proud when I called. I don't understand –

ROSS. In my century, what you just did is called snooping.

AVINASH. You've misunderstood my –

ROSS. Avinash. I don't want you for a friend. I don't want you for a boss. I'm trying to do my job in a less than satisfactory environment. Just let me do my job, okay?

AVINASH. There is a power outage in Wrigleyville. Also all the phone lines are down in Brown County. Avoid Brown County accounts till noon. I've e-mailed you the updates.

I'll be watching you very closely, boy. I want you to know that. I'll be listening to every word you speak.

ROSS. Okay. I'll – I'll keep it in mind. Yeah. Yeah.

AVINASH. The break's up.

AVINASH leaves. ROSS waits till he's sure AVINASH has left. He turns to the window. He picks up his cellphone and calls furtively.

(*Into cellphone.*) Sara, hi, it's me. Sorry it took me so long.

Did you call 911?

Listen to me, listen to me – Forget the money. You're safe, that's what counts. Okay?

You're a brave woman.

Now. Did you call 911?

I want you to call them, okay? Shall I do that –

Promise me you'll call. You can get a restraining order against him. It's America, Sara. People have rights in America.

Don't cry. It's going to be all right. I'm there for you.

Me too. Sara, if only you knew...

Listen, Sara – this is my cellphone. Save my number.

Any other number, you have to be very careful what you say.

Yes, only official things.

You can't say that.

You can't say that either, Sara.

You could say... 'I hear you.'

I hear you too, Sara.

Scene Seven

ROSS *is surreptitiously keying some figures into the computer.*
GIRI*'s computer monitor shows a funky black-leather jacket.*
GIRI*'s call can be loud or soft as the situation demands.*

GIRI (*into mic*). I'm sorry you are going through a trying period.

But I don't get it. You spent over $6,000 when you knew you wouldn't be getting a monthly cheque.

VIDYA (*into mic*). I'm sorry you are going through a trying period.

When you can pay –

Can you borrow it from someone? Your mother, your family?

Beep.

GIRI. Let me get this straight. You say you lost your job and you shopped for a D&G jacket, a Sony big-screen, an Xbox, Calvin Klein underwear and a pair of rollerblades immediately after.

VIDYA. Hi, I'm Vicki Lewis. I'm calling regarding your Helium credi –

Beep.

VIDYA *screams in frustration.*

GIRI. I don't believe you can shrug off your responsibility to our company that easy.

ROSS *is still working on the computer.*

We cannot clear today's transaction unless you clear outstanding dues now. Even if it's for blood-pressure tablets.

VIDYA (*off mic*). Hey, Ross. Isn't only Uncle allowed to run this software?

ROSS *jumps, quickly switches screen.*

ROSS. None of your business.

VIDYA (*into mic*). Hi, Mr James H. Bennet. I'm calling about your cheque –

When did you mail it?

Was it by priority?

Do you have the cheque number?

If you have your chequebook with you, we can –

I suggest you issue us another one –

I can only wait for one more day, Mr Bennet. That's it.

Beep.

GIRI. Do you have your bills with you for all the things you bought that you shouldn't have?

Pause.

VIDYA (*off mic*). Ross. I got you something – a a token. It's in your drawer.

ROSS *hesitates.*

GIRI. Yes, for your jacket, your Xbox, the lot. Do you have them with you now?

VIDYA. Aren't you going to take a look?

(*Into mic.*) Hi there. Is your mommy at home, honey?

Where is she?

Yes, right now.

Yes, right now right now.

(*Cheerfully, off mic.*) I thought we could do a movie this weekend? What do you –

ROSS. This is not the time or place for –

VIDYA. I don't get to see you –

GIRI. I'll call back in five minutes –

No no no, don't put me… on hold.

VIDYA. We can do dinner after.

(*To* GIRI, *loudly*.) Nailed him?

GIRI (*off mic*). Bastard's wasting my time.

VIDYA (*into mic*). Hi, honey. Is your mommy still in the shower?

Is your daddy at home?

Can you fetch him for me?

ROSS (*re: the picture on* GIRI*'s monitor*). That's a neat jacket.

GIRI. Yeah. I know.

ROSS. Vidya loves leather.

VIDYA. Can you go and get your daddy?

ROSS. Vidya wants to do movie and dinner.

GIRI. Cool. I could book three tickets now and –

ROSS. With you.

GIRI. Me?

VIDYA (*playfully*). I can still hear you.

GIRI (*into mic*). Did you find the bills?

No, keep looking. Just – calm down and look, okay?

It's fine. I'll call back.

Beep.

VIDYA. I can still hear you!

GIRI (*off mic, to* ROSS). You mean, like a…?

ROSS. Yes.

GIRI. Like, me and her?

ROSS. Yes.

VIDYA. Please, honey, go fetch your daddy for me, okay?

GIRI. And you are fine with it?

ROSS. Yeah.

GIRI. I thought....

VIDYA (*into mic, stern*). Where's your daddy?

Okay, I'll – um – call again. Thank you, honey, have a nice day.

Beep.

A pause before VIDYA *bursts out laughing.*

GIRI. What?

She is in hysterics.

VIDYA (*off mic*). He was – he was –

GIRI. What?

VIDYA. He was in the shower with her!

GIRI *laughs too.*

GIRI. Wow.

VIDYA. Yeah.

GIRI. Cool.

VIDYA. That was priceless.

GIRI *laughs, over-brightly.*

What?

GIRI. It's fine by me, you know.

VIDYA. What is?

GIRI. The movie?

VIDYA. Sorry?

Both look at ROSS *for direction.*

ROSS. Aren't you going to give it to him?

VIDYA. What?

ROSS. She's got something for you.

VIDYA. Ross. What are you –

ROSS. She's shy –

VIDYA. Ross, stop it. It's not yours to give –

ROSS holds out a gift-wrapped box to VIDYA.

ROSS. So, give it yourself.

Pause. VIDYA *doesn't move, so* ROSS *gives it to* GIRI.

Aren't you going to open it?

GIRI *wants some direction from* VIDYA, *but she's put on her headset.*

The two of you will hit it off. You're a bit alike. (*Laughs.*) And he doesn't mind dark girls.

Stunned silence.

GIRI. Man, that's not the word –

VIDYA. How considerate of him.

GIRI. He's just kidding, Viddy.

(*Into mic.*) This is Gary again. Have you found the bills?

ROSS (*to* VIDYA). Don't go through my things again.

VIDYA. I didn't go through your things, moron. I just kept that watch in your – Know what – you are a bastard, Ross. You're a cowardly, selfish, spiteful bastard.

| VIDYA (*into mic*). Hi. Is this Harry Coltrane? We spoke last week? You have outstanding dues of \$38,000. | GIRI. We can salvage something of the mess you've created. We can save you from yourself. Here's what I suggest you do. Return them all. |

AVINASH *goes to the coffee machine.* ROSS *puts on his headset, gets on a call.* GIRI *changes screen. Calls become much louder.*

VIDYA. It includes late fee and interest.	GIRI. No, not the – not if you've used the under-wear –

VIDYA. I'll stop it, I'll stop calling if you pay up. Simple.	ROSS (*into mic*). When can I expect a bank transfer?	GIRI. That's not what I said.

AVINASH *fills two cups with water. He looks at the white-board. He surveys the three. They get aggressive with the calls.*

VIDYA. I'm sick of your excuses. Can you or can you not write us the cheque now? I don't care how you get it. You've been sending us on a wild goose's chase for months. Enough of excuses.	ROSS. That's good. That's good. I'll follow it up here. Thank you for using Helium credit cards. Have a good weekend.	GIRI. Return them, get the cash and pay us. Simple. Yes, even the jacket. I urge you return them. I'll call back in the evening, Lucas. Thank you for using Helium credit cards. Have a nice day.

VIDYA. Well, that was Ross and this is me.

I don't care what he said –

I don't know how you get it, as long as you get it, Mr Coltrane.

GIRI (*to* AVINASH). The mark's capitulating. I'll get a Promise to Pay.

ROSS (*to* AVINASH). Mine's dicey. But I'll nail him.

VIDYA. You made a promise. It's time you come good on them. Do you want your sons to know you're a liar and a cheat? Because if you don't pay up, that's what you are.

Stop crying. Be a man. Be someone your sons can be proud of.

Beep.

VIDYA *takes off her headset.*

AVINASH. You sound hoarse. Do you have a cold?

VIDYA (*off mic*). You've got a rasping voice yourself. I don't go around asking you if you've got a cold, do I?

AVINASH. $5,000 more to collect today. Come on, team. (*Claps.*) Go, go, go.

The three put on their headsets again. AVINASH *exits. They take off their headsets. Pause.*

GIRI (*to* VIDYA). I'm sorry if –

VIDYA *has exited.*

You can be such an asshole, know that?

Whatever it is between the two of you, leave me out of it. That's all I want to say.

GIRI *clicks his computer. The jacket reappears onscreen.* ROSS *quickly completes work on his computer.* GIRI *takes out his credit card from his wallet.* GIRI *contemplates his card.* ROSS *has a huge smile on his face.*

Scene Eight

GIRI *has just finished a call. He gets up to enter his figure on the whiteboard.*

ROSS (*into mic*). Hi, Sara? This is Ross, your friend from True Blue Capital.

How are you doing?

This is an official call.

'Thank you.'

You do realise your outstanding balance is $23,046?

$23,023 was two days ago. Plus the late charges.

VIDYA. Giri. What do the marks think when they get calls from us?

GIRI. Sorry?

ROSS. Sara, this is what I've done for you. I ran your account through our software, and guess what? We've forgiven your debt. All you have to pay is $23.

VIDYA. What do you think the marks think? I mean, about us, collectors.

GIRI. I don't know.

ROSS. Now do you feel better?

VIDYA. Do they imagine us when we talk to them? Do they imagine me?

GIRI. Possibly.

ROSS. Sara, Sara – listen. Please remember, all conversations are being recorded to check quality.

VIDYA. Imagine my voice.

ROSS. Let me assure you that at True Blue, we only have the interests of our golden customers at heart.

VIDYA. Then imagine me.

ROSS. Exactly.

VIDYA. Do I sound like my voice belongs to a white person or a dark person –

GIRI. I…

ROSS. I… 'hear' you too, Sara. Very much. From the depths of my soul.

We'll speak soon. Very soon.

VIDYA. I think they see dirty brown people in rags who took away jobs that no American wanted in the first place and are now taking away their money.

ROSS. 'Thank you.' For using Helium cards. Have a great day! (*Laughs.*)

VIDYA *has overheard that.*

VIDYA *goes back to her seat.* VIDYA *ignores* ROSS.

GIRI. You look happy. Nailed?

ROSS (*off mic*). No. What's that?

GIRI. Party whistles.

GIRI *rips open one package.*

VIDYA (*into mic*). I'd like to speak with Harry Coltrane, please.

ROSS *takes a whistle and blows lightly. A colourful strip of paper tongues out of it.*

GIRI. Shh. Try this one.

ROSS *tries.*

VIDYA. He's expecting my call.

ROSS. Neat. Just like in *Archie* comics.

GIRI. Imported, dude. From China.

VIDYA. I don't believe you, ma'am. I think he's avoiding us.

ROSS. Stock up heavily on food and booze.

GIRI. Well, duh.

VIDYA. Please don't yell, ma'am. I'm only doing my –

ROSS. Seriously, man. In parties, you can never have enough food and booze.

VIDYA. Please can you quit crying and tell me, clearly, what exactly is the problem?

GIRI *is ripping open another package.*

ROSS. A jacket?

GIRI. The jacket. Original D&G patented leather.

VIDYA. I don't –

GIRI. It came this evening.

VIDYA. This cannot –

GIRI. The security guy said, 'Isn't it too hot for this?'

VIDYA. When –

GIRI. I said, 'It gets cold in Illinois.'

VIDYA. When did this happen? Look I –

ROSS *blows again.*

My sincere condolences, Mrs Coltrane. I'm –

Beep.

I'm so sorry.

VIDYA *is in shock. She removes her headset.*

They laugh. GIRI *puts the jacket on and shows off his boots too.*

GIRI. Italian. Gucci. (*To* VIDYA.) What do you think?

VIDYA *nods.*

ROSS. Must have cost a month's salary.

GIRI. That's why we use a card. (*Laughs.*)

ROSS. Canteen?

VIDYA (*off mic*). Ross…

GIRI *and* ROSS *exit.*

VIDYA *sits, still, silent, begins to weep quietly.*

Scene Nine

AVINASH *is eating a sandwich.*

VIDYA. Hiya. May I come in? Your log said 'dinner break'.

AVINASH. Collections good today?

VIDYA. $700.

AVINASH. Vidya.

VIDYA. I still have six hours left.

AVINASH. Then you'd better get on with it, don't you think?

AVINASH *fills a styrofoam cup with water and pours into the cacti pots. Two cups per pot.*

VIDYA. You don't need to drown them in water.

AVINASH. It's only two cups. That's too much?

VIDYA. Absolutely. One cup should do, I'll say.

AVINASH. Oh.

VIDYA. Every week or so.

AVINASH. Oh.

VIDYA. The key is not water but sunshine. I googled. There's a lot of stuff you can find out. You just need to use the right words.

AVINASH *takes away the cup without watering the cacti.*

Do you miss sunshine? It's my break too. So. Do you miss it?

AVINASH. Don't you?

VIDYA. No. Keeps me fair-skinned. Maybe if I work here long enough I can become white. (*Laughs.*)

AVINASH. Why would you want that?

VIDYA. Everyone does. Wouldn't it be great if we could choose the colour of our skin, the tone of our voice, the colour of our eyes? Like, from a catalogue.

AVINASH. Or the type of personality. My daughter thinks I'm gloomy.

VIDYA. I hate Angelina Jolie. Like, I'd choose someone like, I don't know, like Barack Obama maybe? Only white and female.

AVINASH looks at his watch. VIDYA hands him a box.

I got you this. It's nothing really.

AVINASH. An ultraviolet lamp. You needn't have –

VIDYA (*re: the cacti*). For them.

AVINASH. That's very kind of you. Thank you.

VIDYA. Because there are no windows and they do need a lot of UV for chlorophyll and all that.

AVINASH. How much should I –

VIDYA. It's nothing. It's dirt cheap. Really. It's okay. It's a gift.

AVINASH (*laughs*). The Chinese think of everything.

VIDYA. Yeah. Yeah.

They look at the box on the table.

AVINASH. Right.

VIDYA. Aren't you going to open it?

AVINASH opens the box and pulls out the lamp. He pulls out a sheet of paper with diagrams.

AVINASH. The instruction is in Chinese.

VIDYA *laughs*.

VIDYA. You crack me up. Who reads instructions? Look at the picture. This is how it should look. So just go about fixing it so it looks like it should.

AVINASH *tries to fix the lamp*.

You should come back to the hot seat, the swear words get dirtier and dirtier every day. As if I'm a thief after their money. I'm like, 'It's not your money, you moron. It's ours.' They don't get it. They don't get the concept that you got to pay for the stuff you buy off of your card.

AVINASH. Don't take it personally. If they yell and swear, remember they're not doing it to Vidya. They're doing it to Vicki.

VIDYA. What the hell is the difference? I mean, Vicki's white, blonde and all that. But she's me. I'm her. I can't make that distinction like Giri or Ross. They put on the collector hat and they become someone else. I'm me. Always me. I can't run away from me. Because I'm always after me. (*Laughs*.)

VIDYA *takes the pieces from* AVINASH *and begins to fix the lamp*.

My father doesn't like me working here. I had to fight with him so I could work here.

AVINASH. I have a daughter almost your age. I wouldn't like her to do nights either.

VIDYA. That's so last century. This is a job, it's a good, respectable, rewarding job.

(*Pause*.) Do you... do you suppose voices can kill people?

AVINASH. Didn't Sirens kill? Didn't they lull the poor sailors with their songs and then finish them off? What some voices can do is break glasses – I don't know if that's a myth too.

VIDYA *finishes installing the lamp. She plugs it in and switches it on.*

It works.

VIDYA. Of course it does. You got to point it at the plants. Like in the picture.

AVINASH. Thanks.

VIDYA. No problem. (*Pause.*) Well. Then. I got to go.

VIDYA *doesn't leave.*

You said we should do our job and not worry about the marks.

AVINASH. Yes.

VIDYA. You said they're at fault for being in debt. Didn't you?

AVINASH. Yes.

VIDYA. I did my job.

AVINASH. That point is moot if you've only collected –

VIDYA. A mark died last week. Harry Coltrane. Ross's mark. He shot himself in the head an hour after a collector had called him. That collector was me, Avinash. I was the last person in the world he spoke to.

Silence.

AVINASH. You can't be sure it was you. Perhaps there were other collectors.

VIDYA. There were. He had six different credit cards. He was up to here in debt. He died at 3 p.m. I called him at 2 p.m. It was me.

AVINASH. You didn't pull the trigger.

VIDYA. I caused him to. We caused him to.

AVINASH. He caused himself to. He created the circumstances. He is responsible. Not you. Understand? He was a weak man with a big debt. Not your fault.

VIDYA *nods*.

VIDYA. He died an hour after I called. Avinash. I… blast it all.

VIDYA *tries not to cry*.

AVINASH. You've got to put this behind you. You've got another six hours of collections to do.

VIDYA *nods*.

These things happen. You have to learn to take it in your stride. It's a job. We are collecting, not doing anything criminal.

VIDYA. Maybe we should have let him go.

AVINASH. It wasn't our decision. Bob holds all the strings. Bob didn't want us to. Vidya, we are not a charity. We are not authorised to help people. Coltrane didn't manage his finances. He didn't organise his life. He didn't prioritise. He is to blame. I want you to forget this and focus on the other marks. Vidya, don't get so emotional. The death is unfortunate. Snap out of it. Vicki has a job to do. All right?

VIDYA *hugs* AVINASH. *He's shocked*.

VIDYA. Please.

AVINASH *accepts the hug. He pats her on the head*.

I'm not a puppy.

AVINASH. I…

VIDYA. I'm not your daughter.

VIDYA *kisses him*.

GIRI *and* ROSS *enter*. GIRI *has his money jar. They see* AVINASH *and* VIDYA *together*. GIRI *shakes his jar so it jiggles noisily*. AVINASH *breaks away, scandalised*.

AVINASH. I, I, I want you to stop whining and carry on with the job. No more breaks today. Now, please leave. Your break is over.

VIDYA *is about to exit.*

Did you extract a Promise to Pay from the Coltrane family?

VIDYA. What? No.

AVINASH. Do it.

VIDYA. Avinash?

AVINASH. No excuses. A job is a job.

VIDYA *leaves. Awkward silence.* GIRI *jiggles his jar. A pause.*

She – she's in a bit of of a…

GIRI *jiggles his jar.*

Oh, yes. The party.

AVINASH *pulls out his wallet and puts in a hundred rupees.* GIRI *jiggles again.* AVINASH *pulls out another hundred rupees and inserts it in the jar. When* GIRI *doesn't move, he pulls out three more notes and puts them in the jar.*

Scene Ten

GIRI *enters with parcels.* VIDYA *goes to the whiteboard to enter her figure.*

GIRI. Have you been to the mail unit in the basement?

ROSS. No.

GIRI. The building gives me the creeps. You can easily misplace yourself if you're not careful.

ROSS. It's not so bad. I like this place because it's never dark.

GIRI. Especially not at night, huh?

VIDYA (*to* GIRI). So. Party preparation going well? I read the tweets. Did you?

GIRI *is unable to look at her.*

GIRI. No.

VIDYA. Well they are quite funny, some of them. What's Gary
    going to come as at the party?

GIRI. I don't know.

VIDYA. I'm thinking, Vicki is a very practical kind of person.
    Maybe, maybe she'll come as a as a, I don't know. In a suit?
    That sounds blah, doesn't it, for a party?

GIRI. Excuse me. Work, you know. Target and stuff.

GIRI *puts on his headset.*

	GIRI (*into mic*). Hi, Eric. This is Gary Evans with True Blue.
VIDYA (*to* ROSS) There's this mark who says he's mailed the cheque. It's not reached us. He says it's not his fault and he won't write us another one.	You asked me to call you today.
ROSS. Are you asking me?	Last week, Eric.
VIDYA. Yes.	
ROSS. You could keep calling him and keep asking for another cheque.	You owe $15,600 on your Helium.
VIDYA. So that's what you recommend –	You spend more than you earn. That's the problem.
ROSS. It's in the manual.	
VIDYA. Is there another option?	You must prioritise. Ask yourself, can I do without this?
ROSS. Your boyfriend won't like it.	

VIDYA. My mistake for asking.

ROSS. What's his name? Your mark. (*Pause*.) The one with the cheque in the mail?

VIDYA. James H. Bennet.

ROSS. You could transfer him to me.

VIDYA (*surprised*). Thank you.

ROSS. No problem.

VIDYA. Ross, I…

ROSS. Take notes.

'Ross Adams, Lesson No. 321.' (*Into mic*.) Good morning. Are you Mr James H. Bennet? I'm Ross Adams with the US Postal Service. I've received a complaint from True Blue Capital that a cheque has been stolen in the mail.

Well, I'm calling you because it was your cheque –

Didn't you claim that a cheque for $3,000 was stolen in the mail?

As you know, stealing a cheque is a federal offence. We'd like to let

You can always hang up if you don't like what I have to say.

Thank you.

Your wife wants a responsible husband.

I think it's possible we can make a dent in your debt.

I wouldn't say it if I didn't think so.

The good news is you are better off than most.

You got a job. Your wife and kids are two blocks away.

All you have to do is organise a little.

Let's work it out. What's your monthly paycheque?

Eric? Hello?

Eric, I can easily check my records. It's not a state secret.

Good. Look at your

you know that we are taking your claim very seriously. Federal officers will be visiting your place.

Missing, lost, stolen – we'll decide after the investigation.

Thank you sir.

(*Off mic, to* VIDYA.) There you go. I bet you your cheque will be put in the mail today.

Pause.

VIDYA. We're not supposed to impersonate –

ROSS. He lied, so we lied. Square, in my book.

VIDYA *wants to say more but doesn't.*

monthly bills. How much do you spend every week on food and grocery?

Multiply by four. That's your monthly expenses. Do you have a car? Look at rent. Utilities. Phone bills. How much do they add up?

How much can you set aside every month.

$250 is going to take you forever, Eric. You can do better than that.

Do you really need the car?

ROSS. You and him. When did it start?

VIDYA. There's nothing happening –

GIRI. How many mouths do you have?

How many phones should you have?

That's what I'm saying. Be strict with yourself.

ROSS (*into mic*).	VIDYA (*into mic*).	GIRI. I've
Your outstanding dues on your Helium –	Has your unemployment cheque come in?	discussed your case with my boss and we can make you a special offer. We can waive your
You're saying –	That's right, your Helium	

your wife –

Ex-wife, sorry. She said it was your responsibility.

details will be sent to the credit union.

What it means is the interest rate will shoot up next month. How are you going to dig yourself out of that mess?

finance charges for a year.

It means you'll only have to pay $15,000 in a year.

That works up to $1,250 a month. You can do that.

VIDYA (*off mic*). There's nothing –

ROSS (*off mic*). It's all right, you know?

Pause.

VIDYA. It is?

ROSS. Yeah really. You should have picked someone younger – and single.

GIRI.

Uh-huh.

Uh-huh.

VIDYA. Like Giri?

ROSS. Sure.

GIRI *briefly turns when he hears his name.*

But just so you know, you have options.

VIDYA. Like what?

ROSS. There are many who think girls like you are exotic.

ROSS (*into mic*). No, I've had enough. I've been going back and forth like a

VIDYA (*into mic*). I'm sorry. I wasn't – I didn't

GIRI. I told you it's a one-time offer only.

I've already

ping-pong ball between you two for the last four months. Both of you are the cardholders and so both of you are liable to pay your debt. How are you going to do this?

get that.

I'm listening.

What this means is you'll no longer be eligible to borrow. You'll no longer have any credit card or or or –

given you time.

I can't go lower than that, Eric.

That's our offer.

VIDYA *breaks off mid-call.*

VIDYA (*off mic*). What's going on?

Pause. ROSS *has heard it. He continues with his call.*

ROSS. Or you both simply pay up half. It's simpler.

I've mooted this solution to your ex-wife too.

GIRI. It's going to be a bit tight for a while. But it will be worth it.

VIDYA (*into mic*). Here's what I'm going to do, I'm going to let you think about this and call back asap.

You got to decide, Eric, and fast.

Clean up the mess you made.

A cheque will be great.

Pause. VIDYA *sneaks a peek at* ROSS's *computer.*

ROSS *catches her.*

ROSS. What the hell?

GIRI. Uh-huh.

Uh-huh.

GIRI *is a little distracted by them at this point.*

GIRI. Can you repeat the cheque number, please?

I checked our records. I'll be honest. Your share of the debt is higher.

What can I say, you seem to have expensive tastes in colognes. Her cosmetics are from Walmart.

VIDYA *covers* ROSS*'s mic.*

VIDYA (*off mic*). You're seeing someone.

ROSS (*into mic*). Fuck! Quit that!

GIRI (*off mic*). Lower your voices, please.

ROSS *clicks his computer off.*

ROSS (*into mic*). Sorry about that. In my opinion, I think you should split payment with her. Fifty-fifty. Do you want me to send you the details so you can be absolutely sure?

(*Off mic.*) Don't ever do that again.

GIRI (*into mic*). You've done well for this month. Remember, you have to keep it up for a year and a half more.

ROSS *is about to get back to his call.*

VIDYA. They'd blocked Facebook.	GIRI It's a fantastic first step.
	Yeah.
ROSS. Are you going to tattle to your boyfriend?	
VIDYA. He's not –	
	Yeah.
Since when are you 'In a relationship'?	That's right.
Pause.	Thank you, Eric, for using Helium. Have a great day.
Who is she? Do I know her?	
ROSS (*mock-dramatic*). Do	Hi, this is Gary Evans of

you really want to know?

VIDYA. Yes.

ROSS. Promise me you
won't tell anyone.

VIDYA. I promise.

ROSS. It's… Angelina Jolie.

> ROSS *bursts into
> laughter.*

GIRI (*off mic*). For fuck's sake.

ROSS. Oops.

He puts his finger on his lips.

Angie's my one true love.

He laughs. GIRI *swivels away from* ROSS *and* VIDYA *so he
can concentrate.*

VIDYA. Like she'll have
you. Like she'll go for a
little Indian village boy.

ROSS. I can have Angie like
that. (*He snaps his
fingers.*) I can have any
woman like that. (*He
snaps again.*)

VIDYA. Ross.

> ROSS *presses a key. He
> places his headset on*
> VIDYA.

What are you doing?

ROSS. Talk to her.

VIDYA. To whom?

True Blue Capital.

Did you have a chance to
think about our offer?

$2,500.

That's right.

GIRI. The offer will expire
this evening.

Your debt won't go away.
It will sit with us and
fester.

On the contrary, I'm
trying to help you.

I realise you've been laid
off –

Right.

VIDYA *tries to pull the headset off but* ROSS *is pressing it to her head very tightly.*

Ross. You're hurting –

ROSS. Shut the fuck up and listen.

(*Smiles to* GIRI.) Sorry, dude. We'll shut up.

ROSS *waits till* GIRI *gets back to his call.*

That's my girlfriend. Talk to her. You'll see how special she is.

VIDYA. I don't want to – Ross.

It's her voicemail.

ROSS *snatches away the headset and puts it on. He listens to it as if listening to music.*

ROSS *dials again. He listens again.*

Silence.

VIDYA. Is she a mark? (*Pause.*) How much has she paid us, Ross?

ROSS. She – she's got this soft voice –

VIDYA. How much?

ROSS. She says I remind her

According to our records –

It means $2,500 is not a big amount at all for your partner.

GIRI *turns to* ROSS *and* VIDYA *sharply and glares at them.*

It was only a suggestion.

No, I won't speak with him.

I promise.

My point –

Debt grows, that's what I'm saying.

But it's not too late now.

How much can you pay?

Tell you what? Can you pay $225 per month? We can waive the interest and other charges.

So, $225 a month for eleven months. You'll be in fact paying only of all that's good in life. (*Laughs*.) This is how it should be.

VIDYA (*whispers*). Have you done something? (*Pause*.) Have you, Ross?

ROSS. Stop obsessing about me.

$2,475.

No. $225. It's our final offer.

Excellent. How will you pay?

What's the card number, please?

Thank you very much. Have a great day.

GIRI (*off mic*). I just realised something. I'm the only one here who has to work. You're a supercollector. She's good friends with the immediate boss –

VIDYA. Shut up, Giri. You don't have a freaking clue –

GIRI. And I don't care. I'm tired of it all. I've only had two breaks every day all of last week. Twenty minutes for a ten-hour shift. How many breaks did the two of you have?

AVINASH *enters*.

AVINASH. What is going on here?

Silence. VIDYA *turns her back to* AVINASH.

Giri?

Silence.

Roshan?

Silence.

AVINASH *turns to ask* VIDYA *but she's resolutely ignoring him and fidgeting with her headset.* GIRI *and* ROSS *both watch* AVINASH.

(*Uncomfortable*.) Well. Right.

Everyone adjusts the headsets. They call. It's loud and chaotic. AVINASH *monitors them.*

Scene Eleven

The team is calling. ROSS *has a cellphone in his hand.*

ROSS (*into mic*).
Your Helium
credit card.

Helium.
Helium.

It's a blue and
green card.

Ma'am. Do you
have your credit
cards with you?

You owe us –

You've not paid.

Ma'am. Is your
husband at
home?

(*Into cell*.) Sara,
Ross here. Why
aren't you
picking up your
calls? Please
call me. Please.
I... 'hear' you,
Sara.

VIDYA (*into mic*).
Oh, congratula-
tions on your
new baby. Boy
or girl?

How old is she?

Four months is
a lovely –

This is a
miracle! I mean,
I can see from
my records that
you just had a
baby six months
ago. And just
had another
baby eight
months ago. Are
they quadru-
plets, ma'am?
Because, in the
last one year,
you've had four
babies.

GIRI (*into mic*).
Well, it's a
warm, sunny
day in Buffalo
too. I wish I
could walk out
of the office and
simply sun
myself in the
park for a while.
Like a lizard.

But you could
help me out
here.

You know what
to do.

Make us a
cheque.

You know it's
the right thing to
do.

How much can
you pay?

That's not
acceptable.

I understand,
but –

My boss is not
going to like
that at all.

AVINASH enters with a sheaf of papers. ROSS immediately hides his cellphone.

ROSS (*into mic*). You no pay now, we block card. So you pay. Now.

You no pay, you no use card.

When husband home?

Husband? Could you please repeat it, ma'am?

Please have your husband call me.

VIDYA. Ah. One baby. What's her name?

Lori. That's a lovely name.

How old is she?

Four months... it doesn't add up.

Too right I don't believe you. I don't think there's any baby at all.

GIRI. Much as I'd love to help –

There are rules we got to follow.

I can't agree to something that's this low. I hope you understand.

Why don't you think about what I said? I'll call you again this evening.

Thank you and have a nice day.

During this sequence, AVINASH pretends to go through his papers as he edges close to ROSS and very neatly confiscates the cellphone.

ROSS. My number is 1-800-8687. That's 1-800-U-O-US. My name is Ross. Ross. Ross Adams.

VIDYA. This is your final warning. Tomorrow, information on your delinquency will be sent to the credit union. I can't help if your loans get rejected or if your other cards don't work.

GIRI. I'd like to speak with Mrs –

I'm Gary Evans with –

It's regarding her credit card –

Can you please patch me to her – Thank you.

Hello? Hello?

ROSS (*off mic*). I'm sorry. It won't happen again.

AVINASH. You're absolutely right about that because you're
not getting it back until you reach your monthly target –

ROSS. You fucking can't do that –

AVINASH. This is an office and you'll behave with dignity here.
No dirty words and no cellphones. The team figures are out.
Of the fifty states and Puerto Rico, ours is the lowest. You're
supposed to be the star performer here. Look at your figures.

AVINASH *flings the papers at* ROSS.

You've become plain Clark Kent now.

VIDYA *begins to gather the papers*.

You want to clean the room? That's a better career option for
you.

VIDYA *stops*.

There is $23,000 that's not accounted for, we've not reached
half our target and here you all are chatting on your cellphones during work hours.

Pause.

VIDYA (*off mic*). $23,000?

AVINASH. Yes. Do you know something?

ROSS. Even a moron would know computers are not foolproof.
Software glitches keep happening –

GIRI (*off mic, to cover* ROSS*'s insult*). Oh yeah! Like that time
at your bank – Vidya, tell him. It was funny because she came
to work that evening with bottles of Bacardi because she was
officially a millionaire. Next day she found out they'd
flubbed. They forgot to put in the decimal points. (*Laughs.*)

ROSS (*quietly*). I need my phone.

GIRI. Ross –

ROSS. Butt out.

AVINASH. 'I want.' 'I need.' Is this the sum total of your existence?

Why do you 'need' it?

ROSS. I'm expecting a call.

AVINASH. At this hour?

AVINASH is instantly suspicious. He is about to press a button –

ROSS. Don't.

AVINASH presses the button. ROSS lunges at him and grapples with the older man for the phone. GIRI tries to separate them.

GIRI. Ross, stop it.

The phone breaks.

AVINASH. Is this what they teach you these days? Fisticuffs and brawls at work? I'm shifting you to welcome calls.

ROSS. No. You can't. I'm a supercollector –

AVINASH. Not any more.

ROSS. I'll be wasted in Welcome. I'll die of boredom in Welcome.

AVINASH. Count yourself lucky. If you are fired, you'll get no references from the company. That will be the end. Finding employment with no references is an ordeal, no matter how young you are. While you're in Welcome, think carefully about what you're doing and where you're headed.

ROSS *exits.*

GIRI. He's, uh – he doesn't mean any harm – no, really. He's never done anything like this before. He needs a break, that's all. We all do. He's the one who taught me, you know. Not the trainers. I didn't learn half the stuff I know from them. He's the one who said I got to always package bad news as good news. The attitude is in the voice and all that stuff. It's the stress, Avinash. He'll be fine.

AVINASH. Everyone has the same stress. You can tell your friend, we've decided to cancel all your bonuses.

GIRI. What? Why?

VIDYA. Are you going to penalise us for what Ross just did?

GIRI. I reached my target, man.

AVINASH. No one else did. Knock some sense into your friend. This is work, this is teamwork. One person falls short, everyone suffers.

GIRI. Look, man, we'll get him to apologise. We'll get him to perform. You'll see. We'll make a killing, we swear. We'll rock the next ten days. (*To* VIDYA.) Won't we? Tell him. Just don't do a bonus cut this month, man. I've overextended my credit.

VIDYA. Oh, Giri.

AVINASH. I can't help you here, Giri. I'm sorry.

Maybe if you can get your friends to give us the figures we want, we can reconsider. This is not the old BlitzTel any more. Everyone must pull their weight in here or...

Get back to work.

AVINASH *waits till they put on their headsets and begin calls. He leaves only when the calls are well underway.*

GIRI (*into mic*). Hi, this is Gary. Here's what we can do. We are willing to lower your interest rate to ten per cent from nineteen, provided you write us a cheque for $250.

Yes, you can think about it. I'll call again tomorrow. Thank you and have a nice day.

VIDYA (*into mic*). Hi this is Vicki calling about your Helium. I studied your case thoroughly. Here's what you need to do. You have to pay $450 every month.

You'll have to dip into your savings, Joe.

Discuss it with your father. I'll call in half an hour.

GIRI (*off mic*). I work my butt off and this is what I get. Are you happy now?

VIDYA (*off mic*). That's not fair. I'm trying too.

GIRI. Not enough. Not fucking enough. You're pulling down the team.

VIDYA. Me?

GIRI. He'll bounce back. One good day, and he'll be okay. You – You are sinking us.

VIDYA. You stupid ostrich. You have no idea.

ROSS *enters*.

ROSS. Has he left?

GIRI. Man, he's cut our bonuses.

VIDYA. What the hell have you gone and done? $23,000, Ross. What were you thinking? What were you planning to do? Have a relationship? Marry? What?

GIRI. What are you talking about?

ROSS. We're taking it one day at a time.

GIRI. 'We'?

VIDYA. He and his mark. Tell him.

GIRI. Tell me what?

VIDYA. Tell him how you bought an American girlfriend. Tell him how you wiped her debt.

ROSS. Look, man...

GIRI. You colossal fool, if you're on a suicide mission that's fine, just don't drag me along, that's all. I fucking covered for you, I'm such an idiot, now I'm screwed too, you get it? You've screwed us both. You're such a fuckwit, that's what.

ROSS. I wasn't –

GIRI. Shut up – You could go to prison for this, moron. What if they think I'm your accomplice?

ROSS. Please. It's – We –

GIRI. I don't want to know, okay?

ROSS. It's not –

GIRI. Shut up shut up shut up.

GIRI *exits*.

Scene Twelve

In various accents:

ROSS. Hello. Am I speaking with Ms Sara Johnson? Good morning. True Blue Capital welcomes you as an esteemed customer of its Helium credit cards. It's wonderful to have you as a part of the happy True Blue family.

Beep.

Hello. Ms Sara Johnson? Good morning. True Blue Capital welcomes you as an esteemed customer of its Helium credit cards. It's wonderful to have you as a part of the happy True Blue family.

Beep.

Hello. Am I speaking with Ms Sara Johnson? Good morning. True Blue Capital welcomes you as an esteemed customer of its Helium credit cards. It's wonderful to have you as a part of the happy True Blue family.

Beep.

Scene Thirteen

JYOTHI. Which brings me to point B, a legal notice.

AVINASH. From whom? Against whom?

JYOTHI. We don't have the full. Bob's team will fax us tomorrow.

AVINASH. Do you think it's one of our kids?

JYOTHI. Like, I'm asking you that?

AVINASH. Everyone complains against debt-recovery agents. All credit-card companies must be flooded with legal notices. You cannot take them seriously.

JYOTHI. We really got to. Debt-collection laws and all. Bob was in a, in a – He called an emergency conference.

AVINASH. That's not unusual,

JYOTHI. Like, from his yacht! He likes his personal, you know, space?

AVINASH. What is the notice regarding? What do you know?

JYOTHI. It's a harassment case.

AVINASH. No names?

JYOTHI. Like, Bob was speaking so fast, you know, how Americans (*Slows*.) usually speak so slow. But today, he went like an express train, 'Blahblahblahblah stalking blahblahblah harassment blahblahblah intimidation.' So. Yeah. When he's upset, he so doesn't make any sense.

AVINASH. There are fifty-one teams. It could be anyone, couldn't it? Or it could be none of them.

JYOTHI. If it's Illinois…

AVINASH. It can't be. We have good people in Illinois.

JYOTHI. Avinash, you don't seem to understand. I put my, you know, ass on the line by not… Your team figures are very low. Now this. God, I made a.

AVINASH. Jyothi, you're panicking unnecessarily. Likely, it's a hoax. The mark is pretending to be harassed so they can milk some money out of us. Sometimes, offence is the best form of defence when you are asked to pay up. We've just got to be prepared to fight it out.

JYOTHI. I don't want to have to, you know? Like, fight.

AVINASH. Let's – let's look at what we do know. What do we know?

JYOTHI. Right. Like, the mark is from Springfield. We are waiting for clarification regarding the state.

AVINASH. There are so many Springfields in the country.

JYOTHI. What if it's our Springfield? God, this is such a messed-up time for a lawsuit.

AVINASH. Jyothi, these things will happen when a big project is up for grabs. I say it's the Filipino company's last-ditch effort to malign us.

JYOTHI. We need to be really really sure it's not one of our, what? 'Kids'?

AVINASH. Jyothi. My collectors may be a little pushy – you have to be when you're pushed to the wall –

JYOTHI. / This is what –

AVINASH. / – but they're intelligent kids. I'll look into the matter. I know the ropes, I know exactly where the loop-holes are. If it's someone from Illinois… I need to look into it.

JYOTHI. The management wants an objective, third-party investigation. I can't, you know, stop that.

AVINASH. I'll be thorough. Bob will be satisfied. I know what he wants. He's closer to my age. Tell the management to back off, Jyothi. Sometimes, in such cases, you should let an older man handle it.

JYOTHI. Like. Fine. Two days. That's all I can give you. I want a report in my inbox by July the 4th. I want to know A) What exactly happened, and B) Who is responsible.

AVINASH. Definitely.

GIRI *enters*.

GIRI. You'll be at the party?

JYOTHI. Sorry?

GIRI *jiggles the money jar.*

Yeah, of course!

Scene Fourteen

GIRI *enters wearing a cowboy hat. He sees* AVINASH *and tries to make a quick exit.*

AVINASH. One moment, please.

Pause. GIRI *sits.*

GIRI (*re: the hat*). It's for the party. Don't tell anyone.

AVINASH. Cut the nonsense. What's with Roshan?

GIRI. What do you mean? I don't know much about him, it's quite normal in these workplaces to work next to a person but know next to nothing about him. I'm not a very aware person when I have my headset on, and I do have it on all the time, don't I? (*Laughs.*)

ROSS *has walked past and has seen* GIRI *with* AVINASH.

ROSS *starts to empty his trouser pockets.*

ROSS. See, no cellphones today. Oh. Hey, Giri. I thought you'd left. Vidya was looking for you.

GIRI. If that's all –

AVINASH. Sit.

GIRI *sits*.

ROSS (*to* GIRI). Good doggie. (*To* AVINASH.) I felt energised today. I feel I'm ready to go back to the hot seat, I feel I'm back in the game.

Pause.

AVINASH. Who is Sara?

ROSS (*looks at* GIRI). Who?

AVINASH. Sara Johnson.

ROSS. Sara... Sara... I don't know. I mean. Is she a mark or an alias? What has he been telling you?

GIRI. Nothing – (*To* AVINASH.) Because I don't know what he's talking about –

AVINASH. Thick as thieves, eh?

GIRI. No no no, I'm a regular guy, not a a a, I'm not that stupid, I mean, I'm not that clever, I keep to the script, not that he doesn't, I mean, I don't know if he does or doesn't –

ROSS. We are buddies, aren't we, pal?

GIRI. But not thieves.

AVINASH (*to* ROSS). Who is she? May I jog your memory? You went and donated $23,000 to her as if it were your father's money – don't look at him, look at me.

ROSS. I told you, that was a software malfunction. It's happened before, hasn't it, Giri? Fucking tell him, man!

GIRI. I don't know computers.

ROSS. Okay. Okay. Let's, let's – let's get this cleared. You've obviously got the wrong idea about the the – First, I don't hack. It's not easy, this hacking thing. It requires genius.

AVINASH. It requires deviant minds.

GIRI. I studied English, man. I don't –

ROSS. I'm not dev –

AVINASH. QUIET! Get it in your thick skull that I've reviewed all your calls.

ROSS. All?

AVINASH. You broke more rules than I knew existed, you fool. Why? WHY?

ROSS. You can't make money by following the script. There is no formula for collecting. You've got to play it by ear, you've got to invest something, a bit of yourself, you've got to be creative. I tried to be a good collector.

AVINASH. Do you know what he did?

GIRI. No, no –

ROSS. I... I wanted to help.

AVINASH. This Sara is certainly grateful. (*Reads.*) 'Causing a telephone to ring or engaging any person in telephone conversation repeatedly or continuously: with intent to annoy, abuse, or harass any person at the called number.' The woman has filed a lawsuit.

GIRI. Fuck.

ROSS (*shocked*). Sara?

AVINASH. Yes.

AVINASH *shows* ROSS *the fax.*

Read it!

Silence.

ROSS. There must be some mistake. She... We...

AVINASH. What did you think she'd do if you called her one hundred and sixty-seven times in the past week?

GIRI. Jesus.

AVINASH. If you'd made that many calls to me, I'd sue too.

ROSS. She wouldn't do this to me. She...

ROSS *is shattered*.

AVINASH. What did you expect?

ROSS. We were in a relationship.

Pause.

AVINASH. They are different people from us, Roshan. You have never understood that. (*To* GIRI.) Did you know about this?

GIRI. I – that's a difficult question to to –

ROSS. No. He didn't.

AVINASH. This is it. Clear your desks, put away your hat. The right thing to do is to inform Jyothi.

ROSS. Man, don't... Rajan, my brother... Please.

Silence.

GIRI. What's going to happen?

AVINASH. I – I don't know. I, I, need to think. (*To* ROSS.) Lie low, don't call this Sara woman, not one single phone call, don't do anything. Understand, Roshan? Don't do anything. (*To* GIRI.) You. Not a word.

GIRI *nods*.

Scene Fifteen

4th of July party. Music in the background: 'Born in the USA' by Bruce Springsteen.

ROSS *is dressed in a sequined rock-star outfit and a hat.*

VOICE (*off*). Hey, Gary, where's the booze, man?

AVINASH. It's only a matter of time before the papers sniff this out. Then other debtors will jump on the bandwagon. Then it's a bloody class-action suit.

ROSS (*subdued*). I can explain it to Bob.

AVINASH. 'Explain'?

ROSS. He knows what kind of ungrateful creatures American women are. He's had six girlfriends since I joined. He'll understand.

AVINASH. His company has just got embroiled in a lawsuit. He's not going to be exchanging girlfriend notes with you.

GIRI'S VOICE (*off*). Excuse me. Excuse me. Move up, people. Make way for the booze!

ROSS. Her boyfriend has a Merc. I found out she has a boyfriend who has a Merc. It's her boyfriend who's behind all this. I just know. I'm gonna give her a taste of her own medicine.

AVINASH. No! This is not war. You'll do this peacefully and calmly.

ROSS. Do what?

Silence. AVINASH *holds his head in his hand.*

Do what, Avinash?

AVINASH. Call her.

ROSS. Excuse me?

AVINASH. Call Sara Johnson and get her to retract her complaint.

ROSS. You got to be kidding. (*Pause.*) She won't pick up her phone. I've been trying –

AVINASH. Then get her to pick up the phone, dammit, and grovel. You are a supercollector. Make her listen to you.

Pause.

ROSS. What do you want me to say to her?

AVINASH. Something. Anything. Make her change her mind.

Pause. ROSS takes the headset.

ROSS. Avinash?

AVINASH. What?

ROSS. Wouldn't that be another call?

AVINASH laughs hysterically.

ROSS puts on the headset. He calls.

VOICE (*off*). Gary! We're out of booze!

ROSS. No one's picking it up. Look, it's the 4th. She's probably out, celebrating.

AVINASH. Try her mobile. You know her number.

ROSS tries.

Pause.

ROSS. What now? Should I keep calling? Because it's already two more calls. What do you want me to do? Avinash?

AVINASH. I don't know, all right? I don't know.

Pause.

ROSS. I have the boyfriend's number.

AVINASH looks up.

I got it from the net! So. Do I...?

AVINASH. Yes.

ROSS. 'Yes' what?

AVINASH. Call him!

ROSS *presses a key.*

VIDYA *enters, dressed as Snow White. She has an empty wine glass.*

VIDYA. Where's Giri?

VIDYA *notices* ROSS *wearing the headset.*

What are / you –

AVINASH. No. He's probably in the in the – he's getting more more – food. Your dwarfs are looking for you too. (*Laughs.*) We'll join you in a moment.

AVINASH *tries to rush her out, but she's resistant.*

VIDYA. Is he working today?

AVINASH. Is that wine you're drinking? Does your father know you drink? May I have the glass, please?

VIDYA. This is a party, and I'll drink if I want to. You're such a buzz-kill.

VIDYA *clutches her wine glass and leaves.*

ROSS (*into mic, in Indian accent*). Hello? Am I speaking to Tom Yates?

I am... Avinash.

AVINASH (*shocked*). What?

ROSS (*off mic*). [Shh.] (*Into mic.*) I'm a supervisor with True Blue Capital. It's about Sara Johnson's complaint –

AVINASH. Lawsuit.

ROSS. Lawsuit.

Yes, attorneys are eloquent –

All I want is to personally apologise to her.

No, wait, wait – I understand – It's Indepen –

I know you're out celebrating, but I really need to speak to her, to apologise –

This has happened on my watch, Tom – may I call you Tom? I feel morally –

I am aware you've been forced to take legal –

Perhaps she should know the extent of Ross's crime.

Some of the stuff –

AVINASH. Information, details –

ROSS. Some of the information I'm about to reveal will be extremely useful to your case.

I'm sorry, I can only disclose it to the to the –

AVINASH. Litigant.

ROSS. Litigant.

Silence.

AVINASH. [Is she there...?]

ROSS *shakes his head, unsure.*

Silence.

Then suddenly, ROSS *is overwhelmed. He tries to compose himself.*

ROSS. Hello, Ms Johnson.

Pause.

I'm...

AVINASH *shakes* ROSS.

AVINASH. Get a grip.

ROSS. I'm Avinash from True Blue Capital's call centre in India.

AVINASH. Apologise.

ROSS. I'd like to say how sorry I am for all the pain –

AVINASH. Emotional trauma –

ROSS. Emotional trauma caused by one of my employees.

I regret everything that's happened. I understand that he's been bothering you at work and –

AVINASH. Harassing –

ROSS. Harassing you. I won't go as far as to say 'stalking' –

AVINASH (*hisses*). Roshan –

ROSS. 'Stalking' is the appropriate –

It's a sad, messy affair, and I want to assure you –

AVINASH. We're taking punitive action –

ROSS. We're taking punitive action against this boy. Ross Adams. His conduct is unforgivable and we at True Blue do not condone such blatant violation of your rights. We assure you this will never happen again.

I hope you'll find it in your heart to forgive – No, don't! Wait – just one moment, please.

We have already suspended him. We've filed a case against him according to the Indian penal code. He has been punished by us and he will be punished by the law. What more do you want done against him?

Are you talking compensation here?

AVINASH. Company – lives will be destroyed.

ROSS. In that case, it's my duty to let you know that there are five hundred other lives that will be affected – yes, our company employs –

These are very young people, Sara – Ms Johnson. Barely out of college. Their future will be –

Sara – no, wait.

You'll be destroying a young man's life – is that what you want? You'll be destroying his family – They depend entirely on the salary he sends home. This job is important to him. With the lawsuit, he'll never find employment again.

He made an error in judgement, he thought himself in love.

Ma'am. Those calls, he only wanted to hear your voice. Even if it was just an answering machine.

Pause.

Ma'am, this boy has been known to play with the figures. He's rescued a few –

AVINASH. A few?

ROSS. A few truly indebted Americans. We lose this boy, Helium defaulters will probably lose their only real... friend. You wouldn't want that, would you?

Pause.

You may be aware that he's tampered with your documents –

Yes, it's a crime –

Just the opposite, in fact. Your debt should never have been written off.

You heard me. Yes, ma'am. We have proof.

If you withdraw the lawsuit, we'd consider your account closed and your debt cleared.

I think it's a great idea. You don't have to pay your attorneys – all parties are happy – it's a win-win deal.

Pause.

You've done your homework well. Then I suppose you are ready to take on True Blue. You'll have to fight a battery of the best attorneys in the country – and they can afford the legal fees. Can you?

Pause.

He may not charge you a cent now, but later you'll have to cough up. Look, Sara, just think one moment. What are you going to gain from this? You'll have to pay your debt – yes, we'll do that – plus late fees and interest plus the legal fees. You know how long cases like these take?

Pause.

Please drop the lawsuit. The boy's been punished. His family has been punished –

Pause.

Listen only to your conscience. Whatever the boy did was out of misguided love for you.

Pause.

Don't listen to him – you aren't Erin fucking Brockovich. You don't mess with a lion like True Blue and get away unscathed. You have zero debt now, let's leave it at that. Let's not get too greedy.

Pause.

Will this man you seem to take your advice from still love you when you lose the case? Think about it.

Pause.

Did you enjoy the Cayman Islands, Ms Johnson? It's not exactly a cheap vacation, is it?

If you could have afforded the vacation, you could have cleared your debt.

Did you even call 911?

Did Tom batter you at all?

Do you have a rock band?

Was everything a lie, Sara? I heard you the first time.

I'm Avinash.

Yes, Sara. I'll let our attorneys speak with yours, if that's your decision. But remember, a debt owed is a debt owed, no matter what the outcome of the suit. Sara, your debt will be $24,888 inclusive of interest and late fee.

I am Avinash. Thank you for using Helium cards. Have a lovely 4th of July.

AVINASH *slumps*.

Silence.

VOICES (*off, chanting*). Gary, we want booze. Gary, we want booze. Gary, we want booze.

Music.

ROSS *is at work on the computer.*

AVINASH. What are you doing ?

ROSS. Shh. It's all right. I'm making it all right. I'm giving the bitch an international sucker punch.

JYOTHI *enters. She's wearing a cheerleader costume.*

Pause.

JYOTHI. It's me. Jyothi. Or 'Sharon' tonight.

AVINASH (*tries to laugh*). You look very different.

JYOTHI. Do I?

AVINASH. Yes. You look like a a a a – American.

JYOTHI. God. It's not – is it too much?

AVINASH. No – not at all. It's very natural.

JYOTHI. Thank you.

ROSS *has finished. He starts to dance.*

Who are you?

ROSS. Ross, the rock star.

Pause. JYOTHI *looks at* AVINASH.

AVINASH. Avinash?

JYOTHI. No no. You need to come as someone other than you.

ROSS *dances towards* AVINASH *and places his hat on* AVINASH*'s head.*

JYOTHI *joins him.* GIRI, *dressed as a cowboy, enters, a little harried. He sees the group dancing. He dances too.* VIDYA *enters after a while looking for* GIRI. GIRI *turns away and dances with* ROSS *and* JYOTHI. VIDYA *approaches* GIRI. GIRI *turns to her and it becomes a group dance.* GIRI *tries to get* AVINASH *to dance too. He wriggles uncomfortably. Everyone's dancing now, but soon it is clear who is the centre of attention. All stop to watch* ROSS, *who dances as if there's no tomorrow.*

Scene Sixteen

At the window. VIDYA *is finishing a sandwich.* GIRI *enters.*

VIDYA. Giri. Your math sucks, do you know that? This is two days for you?

GIRI. Yeah. Sorry about that. You know how unpredictable family reunions can be.

VIDYA. Seven freaking days, Giri! What were you thinking? Better get to work. We got a new target.

GIRI. Vidya, listen, I –

VIDYA. I'm so glad you're back. We're really short on collectors now.

GIRI. Since the party?

VIDYA. Yes.

Silence.

GIRI. It was a good party, huh? The music and the the the –

VIDYA. Music!

GIRI. Yeah!

VIDYA. What a night!

GIRI. The whistles were a big hit, weren't they?

VIDYA. Yes.

GIRI. We should have had fireworks. I didn't think of fireworks.

Pause.

It was a crap party.

VIDYA. Yes.

GIRI. Sorry.

Silence.

VIDYA. I'm supervisor now. On probation. If the team reaches the target the next two months, I'll be made permanent.

GIRI. That's great.

VIDYA. Don't you go missing again or leaving me in the lurch. Okay? I need experienced voices here.

GIRI *looks away.*

We can do it, we can make it. (*Laughs.*) We don't need Ross.

GIRI. Yeah.

VIDYA. Two early-stagers have quit this week. So you'll have to handle their work as well –

GIRI. Vidya –

VIDYA. Oh, the coffee machine's working again.

GIRI. I got a job. In Gurgaon. I'll be in sales. Proper face-to-face sales. I just came to – collect my things. That's why…

Pause.

VIDYA. Congrats. It's – That's good.

GIRI. Thanks. I have to join next week. It's a great job, it's a great city, there's nightlife there. Proper pubs and stuff. It all happened very fast, you know. I e-mail my CV on a whim and I do an interview the next day. Bam. I get an offer. I feel I'm ready to move on. See the world. Start afresh.

Silence.

I've my resignation letter. Who should I give it to?

VIDYA. Try the management.

GIRI. Vidya, I'm sorry.

VIDYA. Let me not keep you then.

GIRI *exits. Silence.* ROSS *enters.*

ROSS. Where's Giri? I thought I heard his voice.

VIDYA. Ross! What are you –

ROSS *laughs.*

Shh shh.

ROSS. Chill. No one knows I'm here.

VIDYA (*whispers*). How did you get past the security?

ROSS (*laughs*). I have my ways.

VIDYA. Your mom and dad have been frantic. Where the hell have you been? You look terrible.

ROSS. You look pretty.

VIDYA. You have the freaking nerve –

ROSS. Do you – do you know the garbage dump is a lot bigger in daylight –

VIDYA. Sorry?

ROSS. Come here, come here.

VIDYA. Ross –

ROSS. Please.

VIDYA *reluctantly moves closer to* ROSS. ROSS *turns her around to face the window.*

See those little lights there. See them?

They're imported trucks to flatten mountains and mountains of litter.

VIDYA. I don't see anything.

ROSS. I wonder how it would look from a height in the morning? From a plane or something? It'd be colourful, wouldn't it? Like a field of wild flowers?

VIDYA. You've been here all along, haven't you? Hell. You've been in this building the whole time. Answer me.

ROSS. Oooh. Scary voice. Authority suits you.

VIDYA. Your brother went to the government hospitals to see if you were lying there unconscious or dead. He missed his flight and you're happily – living here. You selfish prick. The least you could have done was call.

ROSS. You know what I want now more than anything else? I want to be in Chicago. Chicago River is great in summer. If I were there, I'd be biking weekends along the river. You'd be swimming. And Giri'd be on his yacht. We'd do amusement parks. And trekking and kayaking. The whole nine yards of American life. I'd do Chicago. I'd lose an arm and a leg to do Chicago. I'd do buildings as tall as the sky. It's beautiful weather today, do you know? Perfect for outdoors.

VIDYA. Ross –

ROSS. Warm, not hot, not humid.

(*Looking out the window.*) Would you like a tour?

VIDYA. Of what?

ROSS. My Chicago. You see that? That's the Millennium Park. That whole sweep of land is the park and that wonderful structure is the Bean.

VIDYA. That's the new pile of rubbish, Ross.

ROSS. That's the Crown Fountain.

VIDYA. That's the electric pole.

ROSS. That's the State Street where you'll find...?

VIDYA. Ross. My break time's –

ROSS. I've a pop quiz for you. Just answer this. What important landmark will you find on State Street?

VIDYA. I don't know.

ROSS. You're not trying.

VIDYA. I don't know, okay?

ROSS. Marshall Field's. Ten points to me.

VIDYA. Ross...

ROSS. Marshall Field's. Marshall Field's. Think like a Chicagoan.

VIDYA. Fine.

ROSS. And there's the Sears – not Willis but Sears. That's a beauty of a building.

VIDYA. Enough.

ROSS. Take me back.

VIDYA. What?

ROSS. We made a great team.

VIDYA. You must be joking.

ROSS. You're the boss now.

VIDYA. No –

ROSS. You can, you can. You can do all the stuff you always wanted to do. We could – we could change the script now. That would be fun. Creating templates, creating scripts together. Or just throw away the scripts.

VIDYA. The script is just fine. Ross, you can't waltz in after everything and expect –

ROSS. Look, look. It was a – I made a mistake. I admit it. I won't do it again.

VIDYA. The company is planning to file an FIR against you.

ROSS. I rectified my mistake –

VIDYA. You are a criminal, Ross.

ROSS. We could be on top of the world – You could be – up there. You need me to be up there – I know their world. I live in their world. I'm a perfect escalation collector. Take me back.

VIDYA. How dare you make demands of me?

ROSS. Fact is: You don't connect with Americans the way I do.

VIDYA. No, Ross. I don't think you understand. Avinash and Sharon-Jyothi have lost their jobs. Bob's transferred the New Jersey work to the Philippines. We don't know if he'll renew our existing contract. Because of you. This ship is sinking because of you. And for what? A white woman you've never met?

Pause.

Do you know if she's even white?

Pause.

We could have been a great team. But you fucked up. Get out of here. Go home. Go to your family.

Leave now or I'll call the security.

VIDYA *takes out her cellphone.* ROSS *jumps to snatch it.*

(*Into cell.*) Roshan Prabhu is here. Please come and get him.

ROSS. You're making a mistake. I'm still the best American around.

VIDYA. You brought this on yourself, Ross.

GIRI *enters.*

GIRI. Ross. Hey.

VIDYA. Giri, will you take him downstairs to the security?

ROSS. No –

VIDYA. He is trespassing.

GIRI. Come on, man. (*To* VIDYA.) I have my resignation letter and I don't have anyone to give it to.

VIDYA. You can give it to me.

GIRI *gives her the letter.*

You need help, Ross.

GIRI. Dude, come on.

ROSS (*to* VIDYA). Do you know Chicago River is dyed green on St Patrick's Day?

GIRI. We'll have proper filter coffee outside.

ROSS. Or or there's Picasso sculptures on the streets – on the streets. You might as well have gold statues. Why hasn't anyone stolen them?

GIRI. Or or egg biryani at the tea shop. Bet you've never had a midnight biryani in your life.

ROSS (*to* VIDYA). Tell me. What do you see out there?

GIRI. Nothing.

ROSS. The point is, when it's dark it can be anything.

As ROSS *looks out of the window, he sees the Chicago skyline. The picture gets clearer and clearer. We see the garbage dump.*

We hear a voice beginning to call. Then another voice calling, then another. It's a cacophony of collection calls again.

The End.

A Nick Hern Book

Disconnect first published in Great Britain in 2010 as a paperback
original by Nick Hern Books Limited, 14 Larden Road, London
W3 7ST, in association with the Royal Court Theatre, London

Disconnect copyright © 2010 Anupama Chandrasekhar

Anupama Chandrasekhar has asserted her right to be identified as the
author of this work

Cover illustration: feastcreative.com
Cover design: Ned Hoste, 2H

Typeset by Nick Hern Books, London
Printed and bound in Great Britain by CPI Bookmarque, Croydon,
Surrey

A CIP catalogue record for this book is available from the British Library

ISBN 978 1 84842 085 4

Mixed Sources

Product group from well-managed
forests and other controlled sources
www.fsc.org Cert no. TT-COC-002227
© 1996 Forest Stewardship Council